LALLY KATZ is one of Australia's most performed playwrights. Her plays display a rare and original voice for the stage in works including *The Eisteddfod*, *The Black Swan of Trespass*, *A Golem Story*, *Starchaser* and *Neighbourhood Watch*. Lally started her career making theatre with director Chris Kohn at Stuck Pigs Squealing wherever they could find an audience and created a strong reputation for their work, winning the 2005 Producer's Choice Award at the International Fringe Festival in New York. Lally has developed new work with the National Theatre in England, was a writer in residence at Melbourne University, won the British Council's Realise Your Dream Award and received a Churchill Fellowship. *Goodbye Vaudeville Charlie Mudd* won the Victorian Premier's Award in 2009 and other work has variously won Green Room awards, Sydney Theatre awards and the RE Ross Trust Award.

Neighbourhood Watch

LALLY KATZ

CURRENCY PRESS
SYDNEY

CURRENCY PLAYS

First published in 2011
by Currency Press Pty Ltd,
PO Box 2287, Strawberry Hills, NSW, 2012, Australia
enquiries@currency.com.au
www.currency.com.au

in association with
Belvoir, Sydney.

This revised edition first published in 2014.

Reprinted 2014, 2023.

National Library of Australia CIP data is available from the National Library
of Australia Catalogue: http://catalogue.nla.gov.au

Typeset by Dean Nottle for Currency Press.
Cover design by Katy Wall for Currency Press.
Cover shows Robyn Nevin as Ana in the 2014 MTC production. (Photo: Jeff
Busby.)

Contents

Currency Press acknowledges the Traditional Owners of the Country on which we live and work. We pay our respects to all Aboriginal and Torres Strait Islander Elders, past and present.

Dedicated to Anna Bosnjak and Robyn Nevin

Neighbourhood Watch was first produced by Belvoir at Belvoir St Theatre, Sydney, on 27 July 2011, with the following cast:

KEN	Charlie Garber
MUSICIAN, CHEMIST	Stefan Gregory
CATHERINE	Megan Holloway
MILOVA (now JOVANKA)*	Kris McQuade
MARTIN	Ian Meadows
CHRISTINA (now KATRINA)*	Heather Mitchell
ANA	Robyn Nevin

The remaining roles were played by the company.

Director, Simon Stone
Set and Costume Designer, Dale Ferguson
Lighting Designer, Damien Cooper
Composer and Sound Designer, Stefan Gregory
Dramaturg, Eamon Flack
Stage Manager, Luke McGettigan
Assistant Stage Managers, Mel Dyer and Michael Maclean

---

* In this revised edition playwright Lally Katz made a number of changes to character names. Please see Note on next page.

PLEASE NOTE

Playwright Lally Katz has made three character name changes in this revised edition: MILOVA is now JOVANKA; DOCTOR VALKER is now DOCTOR VHITE and CHRISTINA is now KATRINA.

CHARACTERS

In Australia:

ANA, an 80-year-old Hungarian woman
CATHERINE, a woman in her late 20s
KEN, a man in his early 30s
MARTIN, a man in his late 20s
KATRINA, a woman in her early to mid 50s
JOVANKA, a Serbian woman in her late 70s
NANCY, a woman from 45 to 65 years old
DOCTOR VHITE, a woman in her mid to late 40s
CHEMIST, a man in his late 20s/early 30s
POSTMAN, any age
POLICEMAN, a young man
DOCTOR'S RECEPTIONIST, any age
SAFEWAY EMPLOYEE, any age
WOMAN WITH SMALL DOG, any age
SAFEWAY DELIVERY BOY, a teenage boy
WOMAN WORKING AT CINEMA, any age
AMBULANCE OFFICER, any age

In Hungary:

    ANA'S FATHER
    ANA'S MOTHER
    ANA'S SISTER
    GYPSY
    SOLDIER
    ARTUR
    SOLDIER IN INFIRMARY
    RUSSIAN SOLDIER
    SOLDIER'S MOTHER
    SOLDIER'S FATHER
    MEAN GIRL AT ANA'S WORK
    POLICEMAN IN HUNGARY

CASTING NOTE

Many of the roles in this play are tiny and any actor can play multiple roles.

The Hungarian roles can be doubled by the actors playing the characters in modern Australia. However, consideration should go into this doubling as it will inevitably bleed into the story of the characters in modern Australia (especially the roles that the actors playing Martin and Ken play in the past in Hungary).

LOCATIONS

The play is set mainly on a street in suburban Australia. In this
current script it is in Sydney, Australia, but it can easily be set in
the suburbs of Melbourne, Adelaide, Brisbane, Canberra or any
other Australian city depending where it is performed. The play
has multiple locations, including the outside street, Ana's house,
Catherine and Ken's house, the doctor's surgery, the chemist,
the cinema, and Hungary during World War Two. It is up to the
director and design team to work out the best way to represent
these shifts in location and time.

ACT ONE

SCENE ONE

Mary Street. It is dawn. The dawn light is a sort of thin violet colour, similar to evening, but with the feeling of it rising.

The street is still and quiet, not quite woken up yet.

Only CATHERINE *is out there. She's wearing pyjamas and is sitting cross-legged on the brick letterbox, on the street, out the front of her house.*

She looks out into the street, as though she is a prisoner looking out into the world. Her mobile phone sits beside her. It begins to ring. It rings and rings. She looks at it, heartbroken. But she doesn't answer it.

KEN, *her housemate, in his early to mid 30s, comes outside. He's wearing tracksuit pants and an old jumper. He's carrying a laptop computer. He stands behind her, bemused, but also slightly authoritative.*

KEN: Happy Kevin '07, my friend.
CATHERINE: Happy Kevin '07.
KEN: You're up very early.
CATHERINE: So are you.
KEN: All-nighter.
CATHERINE: Did you win?
KEN: We killed the monster. But we had to spend a lot of gold.

> CATHERINE *looks out into the street.*

CATHERINE: Do you think the street looks more hopeful?
KEN: Why would it look more hopeful?
CATHERINE: Because Labor won the election?
KEN: Governments schovernments.
CATHERINE: What about 'The West Wing'?
KEN: If Jed Bartlet was our prime minister then I'd be excited.
CATHERINE: I wish something would happen. That would change the whole world.

> KEN *sits down, on the driveway, next to the letterbox. He begins to play World of Warcraft on his laptop.*

Mary Street is starting to wake up now. On the other side of the street, KATRINA, *very attractive, well-groomed, in her 50s, comes out the front of her house. She is shaking out a rug, but she is doing it quite feebly.*

A head peeks up over the fence. KATRINA *doesn't seem to see it. And then,* ANA, *80 years old, Hungarian, wearing all maroon, with her golden-tinged hair piled neatly on top of her head, comes out from behind her white picket fence gate, shutting it quickly behind her. She is carrying a bag of leaves. The sound of terrifying dog barking comes from behind the gate.* ANA *makes a shushing motion at the dog.*

ANA: Shht! [*She makes her way over to Katrina's porch, carrying the bag of leaves.*] Katrina, I return these leaves vhich fall from your tree into my yards.

ANA *hands* KATRINA *the bag of leaves.*

KATRINA: Oh I'm sorry Ana, I'll have to get it pruned soon.

ANA: I don't ask for the bother, only return to you vhat is yours.
   You vant help vith the rug? I can bang it and you hold.

KATRINA: That's alright, Ana, I'm just giving it a little shake. It's not too dusty.

ANA: Is too dusty! Should to bang.

ANA *begins to bang the rug, whether* KATRINA *wants her to or not.*

KEN *takes his computer and stands up.*

KEN: I'm gonna have a nap. What are you up to today?

CATHERINE: I've got a lot of ironing to do.

KEN: Again?

CATHERINE: It gets wrinkly.

KEN: You're a freak.

KEN *walks inside.*

CATHERINE *holds her phone.*

Across the street, ANA *is still banging on Katrina's rug. She can hit very hard for an 80-year-old lady.*

KATRINA *coughs and turns her head from the commotion of it.* ANA *speaks in a very polite voice as she bangs.*

ANA: I vant to asking you, Katrina, my Doctor Vhite send me to the very big appointment vith the stomach bowel specialist next veek. They vill put me unconscious for the camera. I vant to asking you can drive me back home?

KATRINA: Which day?

ANA: Tuesday.

KATRINA: I'm sorry, Ana, I'm looking after my grandchildren on Tuesday. Can you catch a taxi?

ANA: No, I must to be picked up by somevone who know me. Doctor said it is the law.

KATRINA: You can hire a nurse for the day, Ana.

ANA: I don't like the nurse. Vorst than Gestapo. Ana never like the nurse.

KATRINA: I'm sorry, Ana, I have to stick to my program.

ANA: Ja. I understand. You are busy vith the grandchilder.

> ANA *is walking down the driveway.* CATHERINE *is walking down her driveway too, onto the street. It looks as if she and* ANA *will meet in the road.*
>
> *Just then the* POSTMAN *arrives. He speaks to* CATHERINE.

POSTMAN: I've got a delivery for number three.

CATHERINE: That's me.

POSTMAN: Just sign here.

> *She signs and then opens the package as she walks inside.* KEN *watches her.*

KEN: What is it this time?

CATHERINE: A kettle.

KEN: Does your mother know that we have two kettles already?

CATHERINE: Yes.

> ANA *comes out of Katrina's gate, onto the street.*
>
> *On the street,* ANA *meets* JOVANKA, *an elderly Serbian woman.* JOVANKA*'s movements are heavy and laboured. She has been dragging herself up the road.* JOVANKA *is very excited to see* ANA.

JOVANKA: Hello, Ana!

> ANA *is not so excited to see* JOVANKA.

ANA: Jovanka.

JOVANKA: I come by bus here to see if you like to have one coffee.

ANA: You should to call first. I am very busy.

JOVANKA: I was calling you, Ana, but you never answering the phone.

ANA: I am very busy vith many friend. Vith many important appointment. That is vhy I am not ansvering the telephone.

JOVANKA: You want to have one coffee?

ANA: No. No coffee. I'm sorry, Jovanka, I must to stick to my program.

JOVANKA: Ja, the program. I will call again tomorrow.

A new day.

CATHERINE is ironing. KEN calls out to her.

KEN: Do you want to watch a lunchtime ep?

CATHERINE: Not right now.

KEN: I'm making sandwiches, you want one?

CATHERINE: No. I've eaten already.

KEN: What did you eat?

CATHERINE thinks for a moment before answering, it's obvious she is lying.

CATHERINE: A sandwich.

KEN: What kind of sandwich?

CATHERINE: I can't remember…

KEN: That's such a pathetic lie. I'm making you a sandwich.

CATHERINE: I hate your sandwiches.

The POSTMAN arrives at the door.

Saved by the bell!

POSTMAN: Delivery. Just sign here.

CATHERINE signs.

CATHERINE: Thank you.

The POSTMAN leaves. CATHERINE looks inside the package.

KEN: Now what?

CATHERINE: A food processor.

KEN: Does your mother know that you can't cook?

CATHERINE: You don't need to be able to cook, the food processor does it for you.

KEN: Uh… yeah.

KATRINA is outside, sweeping her porch. ANA approaches.

ANA: Katrina, I just vake up now from stomach bowel specialist.

KATRINA: So you got someone to drive you? Good.

ANA: Ja, I find.

KATRINA: How are you feeling?

ANA: They put camera right in—very far! They look for everyting! [*She holds out some flower cuttings to* KATRINA.] I bring you from my garden.

KATRINA: Oh, thank you, Ana. Lovely.

ANA: You vant me to show you vhere is good to plant?

> ANA *indicates to the cuttings.*

KATRINA: I was just headed inside to make a phone call, Ana. But thank you.

ANA: Ja. The phone call.

KATRINA: Well, I look forward to planting these.

ANA: Ja. Ve vill see vhat grow.

> KATRINA *hastily leaves.* ANA *heads back to her house.*
>
> JOVANKA *comes trudging up the street.*

JOVANKA: Ana!

ANA: Jovanka.

JOVANKA: I come on the bus. I was calling you. But again no answer.

> *Just then, the* CHEMIST *comes. He's a young man.*

CHEMIST: Hi, Mrs Brajovik. I brought your prescription by.

ANA: Ah! Here is my boy!

> *The Bella, Ana's huge German Shepherd dog, barks and barks, invisibly, from behind the fence.*

No how-how, Bella! [*To the* CHEMIST] Tank you. Tank you. You are the very special boy. Very good chem-ist. Make delivery to the old lady. No-von vill do this but you. How much I owving you?

CHEMIST: Just settle it next time you're in.

ANA: Tank you! Tank you! I vill coming next veek. Ana vill never make the robbery.

CHEMIST: Ha ha, I know! How are you feeling?

ANA: Not too good. I all the time got some problem. I am very allergic to the sun. But no matter. Keep going.

CHEMIST: That's a good attitude. You take care of yourself, Mrs Brajovik.

As he is leaving, the CHEMIST *sees* CATHERINE *coming out of her house, carrying her phone. They catch eyes, but then she looks into her phone.*

ANA: Vait—you vill leave the broken hearts!

CHEMIST: Pardon?

ANA: Your girl. Look how sad she is looking. She tink you forget her. She all the time love you.

CHEMIST: Who?

He thinks that she means CATHERINE, *though they obviously don't know each other.*

ANA: The Bella! Look—she vatching you from back garden, through her fence. Poor sveetheart.

Bella barks. The CHEMIST *laughs and calls out over the fence at Bella.* CATHERINE *is gone.*

CHEMIST: Sorry, Bella! Hello!

Bella barks threateningly.

ANA: Now she is the happy! She all the time liking you.

CHEMIST: I'd hate to see how Bella acts when she doesn't like someone! See you soon, Mrs Brajovik, see you soon, Bella!

The CHEMIST *leaves.* ANA *looks* JOVANKA *in the face.*

ANA: You see, I am all the time busy.

JOVANKA: Coffee?

ANA: No.

JOVANKA: I come again next week. We miss you on Creswick Street, Ana.

CATHERINE *is in the lounge room, rehearsing for an audition. She is reading a script, silently to herself, acting it out.* KEN *is on the computer. He occasionally looks up at her and laughs.*

KEN: What are you doing?

CATHERINE: Rehearsing.

KEN: Did you get a role?

CATHERINE: No.

KEN: An audition?

CATHERINE: No.

KEN: Then why are you rehearsing?

CATHERINE: To stay match fit.

> *A knock on their door. A middle-aged woman,* NANCY, *wearing a tracksuit, knocks on the door.*

> KEN *doesn't answer.* CATHERINE *doesn't seem to notice.* NANCY *knocks again,* KEN *just keeps looking at his computer. She keeps knocking. Finally she calls out.*

NANCY: Yoo hoo, is anyone home? Hello? Are you in there? Yoo hoo!

> KEN *groans.* NANCY *continues to call out through the door.*

Hello, Nancy! Neighbourhood Watch! I'm just going around the street making sure people know about the upcoming meeting—

> KEN *groans and gets up to head to the door.*

> *Outside,* ANA *looks into her wheelie bin and then looks up, the weight of the world on her shoulders.*

ANA: Again! Again vith the dirty nappy! Very illegal. To put the nappy in the bin of the old lady.

> KEN *arrives at the door and speaks to* NANCY.

KEN: I'm sorry. I won't be able to make it.

NANCY: But I haven't told you when it is.

KEN: I'm very busy with my guild. But thank you.

> KEN *shuts the door.*

> NANCY *starts down their driveway. She sees* ANA *is outside.* ANA *is standing over her wheelie bin in anger and despair.*

> NANCY *approaches* ANA.

ANA: Nancy, you got the nappies in your bins?

NANCY: Not today, Ana.

ANA: I know who done. Neighbours on the other side. They got the new baby.

NANCY: Would you like a flier for the next Neighbourhood Watch meeting?

ANA: Ja. Very much the flier.

> *She takes the flier.*

You just been across the street. You know dese young people?

NANCY: No, I'm just doing the rounds.

ANA: That girl all the time standing on the street staring the mobil. Strange tings.

NANCY: You're right to keep track of any small changes that occur in our street, Ana.

ANA: That girl too skinny. Also, I never know, who is belonging dis yellow car? You know who is dis yellow car?

NANCY: I don't recognise it. Perhaps it might be a good idea to write down the number plate.

ANA: Ja. I write.

NANCY: Well done! I hope to see you at the meeting.

ANA: I try. I got the vatersmelon coming. You vant von slice, Nancy?

NANCY: Thank you, Ana, but I have to finish handing these out.

ANA: Perhaps later?

NANCY: I'm busy all day, I'm afraid.

> ANA *waits by her bin, looking disgustedly into it.* CATHERINE *comes outside, mouthing lines to herself. Her phone begins to ring. She doesn't answer it. She goes back inside.*

> *A young* SAFEWAY EMPLOYEE *comes up. He is wearing a uniform and is loaded with bags.*

ANA: You vork for the Safevay? Home delivery?

EMPLOYEE: That's right.

ANA: This is all you bring? I bought many tings.

EMPLOYEE: I've got more in the truck. This is all I could carry at once.

ANA: Tell me, you got my vatersmelon?

EMPLOYEE: Oh yeah. I've got it right here.

> *He is tilting to one side because of the heaviness of the watermelon.*

ANA: Good!

> *She goes over to him, puts her ear right next to it. He is struggling to keep holding it.*

I pick the very good von. All the time I bang it and listen for the sound.

> *She lifts her hand and bangs the watermelon. It makes a thumping sound.*

Very good. You like to having von slice?

EMPLOYEE: I can't, I've got two other deliveries after this one.

ANA: They don't firing you for having the vatersmelon!

EMPLOYEE: I'd better not. But thanks. So these just go in here?

He goes up to the house—a huge sound of barking from the Bella. The EMPLOYEE *jumps back.*

ANA: No matter. I lock her. Then you come.

KEN *and* CATHERINE *are in their lounge room.*

KEN: Lunchtime ep?
CATHERINE: I can't. I'm in character.
KEN: You can't be in character if you're holding the script in your hand.
CATHERINE: No, I am. I really feel this one. I think I'll get this part.

JOVANKA *is knocking on Ana's door. There is no answer.*

JOVANKA: Ana? Ana, hello, Ana? It is Jovanka.
KEN: That weird lady is always knocking on that door.
JOVANKA: Ana? I come for one coffee. Ana?

No answer. ANA *goes into the chemist shop. She gives the* CHEMIST *some carefully counted-out change.*

ANA: You see—I tell you I vill not make the robbery.
CHEMIST: Ha ha, good on ya, Mrs Brajavik!
KEN: When I make my film, then I'll give you an audition.
CATHERINE: For what part?
KEN: The 'you' part.
CATHERINE: Shouldn't I just automatically get it?
KEN: I can't risk it. There could be a lot of actresses out there who do a very good version of you.
CATHERINE: Can you make it a period drama? I've always wanted to be in a period drama.
KEN: No. Any other requests?

KATRINA *comes out onto her porch, in her wig and lovely clothes. She speaks to herself.*

KATRINA: What perfect weather. For everything.

The POSTMAN *comes through.*

POSTMAN: G'day! A letter from your daughter. [*Reading the back of the envelope*] Wow, Hong Kong!
KATRINA: Yes. They're very international.

The afternoon. ANA *is at the reception counter at the doctor's surgery, speaking with the* RECEPTIONIST.

ANA: Four o'clock. I got the appointment vith Doctor Vhite.

RECEPTIONIST: I'm sorry, Mrs Brajovic, but we don't have you booked in for today.

ANA: But I make the appointment. By telephone.

RECEPTIONIST: Are you certain you made the appointment for today?

ANA: I tell you very nicely, I is not the stupid.

The RECEPTIONIST *looks through the appointment book.*

RECEPTIONIST: You've got an appointment for next Thursday at four p.m. Mrs Brajovic. Not today. You've made a mistake.

ANA: I have no made the mistake. Ana never make mistake on such important tings.

RECEPTIONIST: Well, I don't have you in the system for today.

ANA: I vait.

RECEPTIONIST: We're fully booked, Mrs Brajovic.

ANA: I see. Please, give the Doctor Vhite my regard. [*She turns to go. Then to herself*] Vhite.

KEN *and* CATHERINE *are in the lounge room.* CATHERINE *is ironing underwear.*

KEN: It's good you're ironing your underwear—it'll definitely impress all those men you date. Oh sorry, that's right, you don't date anyone.

CATHERINE: It's for myself.

KEN: Imagine if you actually went out on a date, went home with the guy and then took your clothes off and your underwear was unironed? The shame.

The POSTMAN *arrives.*

POSTMAN: Hello. Delivery.

CATHERINE: Hello.

Stepping outside, she takes the package from him and signs for it.

Thank you.

She goes back inside with the package as the POSTMAN *leaves.*

KEN: Your mother is insane.

CATHERINE: This one's for you.

KEN: Yes! [*He opens the package.*] Shit man.

CATHERINE: What?

KEN: Now my mum's sending me stuff.

CATHERINE: What is it?

KEN: A low GI cookbook.

CATHERINE: Oh—could I have a look?

> KATRINA *is outside, sitting on her porch.* ANA *steps outside. She sees* KATRINA.

ANA: Hello, Katrina!

> KATRINA *ducks back inside. The* SAFEWAY EMPLOYEE *comes up to Ana's house.*

EMPLOYEE: Home delivery.

ANA: Tank you.

> *He looks warily at the door.*

No matter. The Bella is lock in backyard.

> *They go inside.*

> *Deep in the evening,* CATHERINE *is sitting on the letterbox. The street is quiet again.* KEN *comes out.*

KEN: How was your audition?

CATHERINE: Oh, it got cancelled.

KEN: But you were working on that for like three weeks!

CATHERINE: How's your script going?

KEN: Touché. Wanna watch a dinner ep?

CATHERINE: I'm not really hungry.

KEN: You okay?

> *There is a flapping sound from high above.* CATHERINE *looks up, into the sky.*

CATHERINE: Yeah. Hey, Ken, look up.

> KEN *looks up.*

KEN: Bats. Cool.

CATHERINE: You haven't seen them before? Hundreds of them fly over here. Every night.

KEN: That's really pretty cool.

CATHERINE: Do you think they're vampires?

KEN: Probably.

KEN *goes inside.*

CATHERINE *is still sitting there, looking at the sky. Her phone begins to ring. She looks at it, achingly, looks away and doesn't answer.*

ANA: Again vith the mobil.

Her head peeks up over her picket fence. She watches CATHERINE. ANA *is wearing rose-tinted seeing eyeglasses. She peers through them at* CATHERINE. CATHERINE*'s eyes meet* ANA*'s.*

Come over here.

CATHERINE *isn't sure if* ANA *means her. She sits up, unsure of what to do, on the letterbox.*

You. Girl. Come. Over. Here.

CATHERINE: Me?

ANA: Vhat, you idiot? No-von else on the street.

CATHERINE gingerly steps off the letterbox. She stands at the curb. It seems as though crossing the street will be like crossing a river.

Yes, yes. Here. On my gate. I showing you someting very important.

CATHERINE *begins to cross the street. When she is halfway across, Bella's barking begins—very vicious.* CATHERINE *stops in the middle of the street, unsure.*

No more, Bella! Listen to mummy. No how-how. No how-how! Ja, come girl. Bella! No how-how!

CATHERINE *walks up to the picket fence.* ANA *is short, her head barely reaches over it.*

How long you been on the Mary Street?

CATHERINE: I've been here for a year.

ANA: Me too! The very same. Von year. I come here from my old street. After my husband die. Von years ago.

CATHERINE: Oh, I'm sorry.

ANA: Yes. He had the cancer. Poor tings.

Vicious barking.

Bella! No how-how! Ja, she vant to kill you. Very dangerous. If the gate do not stop her—she vill be killing you!

CATHERINE: Can she jump the gate?

ANA: Oh, yes. You live here vith von husband?

CATHERINE: No, I'm not married.

ANA: Von boyfriend?

CATHERINE: No.

ANA: Then who is this man I see you vith on the drivevay many time?

CATHERINE: Ken. He's my housemate.

ANA: Housemate?

CATHERINE: My friend who I live with.

ANA: You live vith the man, vith the Ken as friend? Friend?

CATHERINE: Yes.

ANA: But you is attractive girl. Skinny. Good legs. Like Ana vas.

CATHERINE: Who's Ana?

ANA: Who you tink? I am all the time Ana.

CATHERINE: Oh, hi Ana, I'm Catherine.

ANA: Ja, I vas very attractive young girl. You vill see vhat I showing you. This vas Ana.

> *She holds out and old, framed, black-and-white photograph. A young, determined-looking woman stares out. Handsome.*

CATHERINE: Beautiful.

> ANA *nods.*

ANA: Vhy you alvays on the street, staring your mobil? You got some secret from the Ken?

CATHERINE: Oh no—the reception is just better outside.

ANA: Should to be careful who you ansver the telephone to. Perhaps is your enemy.

CATHERINE: My enemy?

ANA: I have many enemy.

CATHERINE: Really?

ANA: Ja. I have many sad story. Von time three men do the pee-pee on my legs.

CATHERINE: Why did three men pee on your legs?

ANA: Because I am the refugee with infection—only vay!

CATHERINE: The only way for what?

ANA: Not for talking on the street. You come inside leetle bit?

CATHERINE: I'm sorry, I can't right now. I'm busy.

ANA: Vith vhat?

CATHERINE: Ironing.

ANA: Good. The ironing important. [*She holds up the picture of herself.*] You see, Ana vas all the time very good dress. *Szervusz* [cheerio], Katerina. Mummy coming, Bella.

SCENE TWO

Inside Catherine's house. It is sort of like a sitcom house. It is all mauve. CATHERINE *is ironing tea towels. When she finishes ironing each one, she folds it, and then irons it folded. And then adds it to a pile of ironed, folded tea towels, which is alongside many, many other ironed items. A lot of ironing has been going on. On the ironing board, sits Catherine's mobile phone too.*

KEN *is sitting at the dining room table, on his laptop. He is staring right into it. He is playing World of Warcraft.*

KEN: I got you a job interview.

CATHERINE: What?

KEN: I'm not trying to push you.

CATHERINE: I'll pay you back the money I owe you.

KEN: I don't care about that.

CATHERINE: I'll start selling Tupperware again.

KEN: You were the only one who ever bought any.

CATHERINE: And now look how organised our cupboards are. I'll probably get a role soon, and then I'll have money.

KEN: My aunt is looking for a waitress at the café she's opened. Fox in the Box. They want to interview you on Friday.

CATHERINE: You don't have a job. Why don't you want it?

KEN: I do have a job. I'm working on my film. I don't know how to waiter anyway. And it's my family. I wouldn't work for my aunt if she paid me.

CATHERINE: Usually no-one works for anyone unless they pay you.

KEN: But I wouldn't. Even if she did. It'll be good for you, Catherine.

CATHERINE: Okay, Ken. I'll do the interview.

KEN: Good. I'm gonna have some insulin now. Do you want some?

CATHERINE: Just a little bit.

KEN: Okay. And then let's watch an ep.

CATHERINE: It's eleven a.m.

KEN: That's lunchtime.

> KEN *prepares his insulin.* CATHERINE *looks into his computer.*

CATHERINE: You've got a dragon now.

KEN: Yup.

CATHERINE: It wouldn't be easy to get a dragon.

KEN: I had to work really hard for it.

CATHERINE: How's your film going?

KEN: Okay.

CATHERINE: Yeah?

KEN: Yeah. Just waiting to hear about money. Still.

CATHERINE: You should tell the investors that you have a dragon. That would really impress them.

KEN: I hadn't thought of that. That's a good idea.

> KEN *brings out some sandwiches. He gets a DVD of 'The West Wing' TV series out.*

We're up to a good one. God, you don't even know what's coming. Oh, man, some shit goes down.

CATHERINE: What happens?

KEN: You think I'm gonna tell you? You have to watch, you little cheat. I will tell you this, though, things aren't looking good for our friend Josh.

CATHERINE: Ohhh…

KEN: Be afraid.

CATHERINE: What does he do?

KEN: You know, normal Josh stuff, but he takes it too far. That's all I'm saying.

CATHERINE: I don't know if I have time.

KEN: Just know that you're only halfway through Season Two. And there's another five seasons after this. You have a lot of work to do. Remember, if you get through to the end of this season by Friday then you can watch at least one episode at my monthly State of Union eps night. Jonathan and Marg are coming.

CATHERINE: I've got aerobics on Friday night.

KEN: That's important. You are starting to look a little fat.

CATHERINE: You think so?

KEN: Don't be an idiot. What are you eating?

CATHERINE: I'll eat after.

KEN: Sure.

She stands there with the ironing. KEN *puts the DVD in the player.*

Get ready for the world how it should be.

Catherine's phone starts to ring.

CATHERINE: Actually, do you mind if we take a raincheck?

She takes the phone with her out of the house. Dejectedly, KEN *takes the DVD out of the machine.*

KEN: And the world how it really is.

SCENE THREE

CATHERINE *steps out into the street, holding her ringing phone. The first thing she hears is a screaming and* ANA *crying out.*

ANA: Bella, inside! Inside, Bella!

A very shaken WOMAN *is cradling a small dog wrapped up in her jumper.* ANA *is at her gate.*

WOMAN: Your dog is a monster!

ANA: I told you—put your dog on the lead!

WOMAN: Why do you have that killer dog in this neighbourhood?

ANA: My Bella vas on the lead—all the time she vas on the lead. I yell to you—my Bella vill eat your Piccolo if he run on her—but you no listen—you don't put your vhite Piccolo on the lead and he run on my Bella—

WOMAN: You should have that monster put down!

The WOMAN *rushes away, cradling her small dog.* ANA *calls out after her.*

ANA: My Bella vas right here—by my side—you should to valk your dog on the lead!

ANA *leans back against the fence, very upset, her wrist dramatically up against her forehead.* CATHERINE *rushes over to her.*

CATHERINE: Ana, Ana, are you okay?

ANA: She vant to kill my Bella.

CATHERINE: Ana, can I help you?

ANA: But should to be on the lead. Piccolo should to be on the lead.

Just then JOVANKA *arrives, coming down the street.*

JOVANKA: Ana! I see! I see what happen.

ANA *speaks under her breath to* CATHERINE.

ANA: Of course she see. Bastard. Ve must to hurry. Inside now.

ANA *and* CATHERINE *disappear into Ana's.* ANA *shuts the door in* JOVANKA*'s face.*

SCENE FOUR

Inside Ana's home. It is beautiful. Everything is water blue and green. There are pictures of frogs hanging up in subtle places all around. The bathroom is blue and green tiles. The back wall of the house is one big, clear window. Out the windows you can see Ana's backyard. Full of flowers. And a huge tree overhanging everything. On the decking there is a cage full of tiny parrots. Sometimes, when the breeze blows, you can hear them singing.

CATHERINE: It's so peaceful here.

ANA: I am upset. I am very upsetly. The Jovanka catch it. All the time she vatching. All the time spying me. When I live on same street vith her, never still the drape of the Jovanka. Vhy she tink I move here? Now alvays coming on the bus. To spying. She vill be saying that the Bella must to be put down—bastard Jovanka. Oh, the poor little Piccolo. I am sorry for the vhite Piccolo.

CATHERINE: I better get going. Will you be okay, Ana?

ANA *stops for a moment.*

ANA: You vant von coffee?

CATHERINE: Are you having one?

ANA: Of course. You make how you like. I make how I like. Final. Final?

CATHERINE: Okay. Final.

ANA: You take the milk?

CATHERINE: What kind of milk?

ANA: Vhat you mean? Only von kind of milk.

CATHERINE: Is it skinny milk, or whole cream?

ANA: Vhat you mean the skinny? The milk is the milk.

CATHERINE: Oh, I don't really need milk.

ANA: Von sugar. You take the sugar.

CATHERINE: Oh, no. I don't have sugar.

ANA: Listen. You make how you like and I make how I like. Final?

CATHERINE: Final.

ANA: And vith it ve take some biscuit. I 'ave the very good biscuit. Softly, softly from the Anzac.

CATHERINE: Oh, I'll just have the coffee. I had a very big lunch.

ANA: Lunch? But the Anzac is not the lunch.

She sits down and leaves CATHERINE *to prepare their coffee.*

Pardon me, madam. Sorry for asking, but I vondering very much, vhy you don't love the Ken who you live vith? He's nice boy, isnt?

CATHERINE: Ken's my friend.

ANA: You vant von other man. Don't lie me.

CATHERINE: I don't know…

ANA: Oh, ho ho. And this von you love, vhere is he? If he love you, vhere is he?

CATHERINE: He left.

ANA: And you vaiting for him. Like idiot! Ana never chase the man, Kitty-kitty. Ana run from the man! Alvays. You must to be busy. Vhat is your job?

CATHERINE: I don't have one right now.

ANA: You is the bludger?

CATHERINE: No.

ANA: Then vhat?

CATHERINE: I'm an actress.

ANA: You are in the television?

CATHERINE: No.

ANA: You are in the film?

CATHERINE: No.

ANA: You are in the tee-at-re?

CATHERINE: No.

ANA: Then vhat?

CATHERINE: I'm going to get a new job soon.

ANA: Good. Ana have three jobs.

CATHERINE: Three?

ANA: Every day for thirty year I am vorking in the Commonvealth bank. Evenings the babysitting. Veekends cleaning the rich houses.

CATHERINE: Wow, you were busy.

ANA: Ja, must to be. Live your life. The man is not so important. Better never to marry.

CATHERINE: But you've been married.

ANA: Tvice!

CATHERINE: Twice?

ANA: That is how I know.

CATHERINE: You didn't love your husbands?

> *As* CATHERINE *makes the coffee,* ANA *begins her story.*

ANA: The second von, Vladir, I love vith all my hearts. He vas the Serbian, but ve click.

> *She looks at* CATHERINE *making the coffee.*

Von sugar, and for me, very much the milk. [*She goes back to the story.*] First time I meet him, forty-eight year ago, he say, 'Hello, Parishka'. You know who dat?

CATHERINE: No.

ANA: Parishka is the Hungarian name of the little von vith the red hood riding. You know dat von.

CATHERINE: Little Red Riding Hood.

ANA: He call me it only tvice in the life. You catch it?

CATHERINE: Yes.

ANA: My Vladir is the good man. The very much gentlyman. Never-never let me to vash his undervears. He tell me, 'No! Vhy should you to vash the popo?' He say to me, 'How I find you? How I find Ana? Out of von million? How I find you?'

Vhen he is in hospital dying, I never leave his side, not for no von moment. I viping his overhead. I holding his hands.

And the time come. Doctor say to me, 'He is going'. I lean to Vladir. I vhisper to him. Doctor say, 'No, he cannot hear you, never anymore'. But still Ana say to him, I say to my husband, 'Do you know who I am?' And he open his eye. Both of. And he say, 'Yes. You are... my sveet Parishka.' And then he die. I close his eye. Both of. Vith my hand. Tvice in the life he call me that. Parishka.

> ANA *leans back in the chair.* CATHERINE *is engrossed.*

CATHERINE: The first time he saw you. And the last time he saw you.

ANA: Ja. Then.

CATHERINE: What happened in between?

ANA: Later. I vill tell later. First I must to ask you, you do me von favour?

CATHERINE: What?

ANA: My bird's cage on back verandah terrible dirty, and vith my old back is very hard to clean all of. You is the young. Vill not hurting you to go, clean leetle bit?

CATHERINE: You want me to clean your birdcage?

ANA: Just leetle bit. Then ve talking more story.

CATHERINE: I've never cleaned a birdcage before.

ANA: You is not the stupid, you can learn.

CATHERINE: Um…

ANA: Sorry to be asking, but you don't got the job and you is not the bludger, you must to have no money?

CATHERINE: I'm okay.

ANA: No money for the rent. For the bills.

CATHERINE: I'm fine.

ANA: I hire you. You is my assistant.

CATHERINE: Better if I'm your friend.

ANA: I give to you von hundred dollar.

CATHERINE: No.

ANA: But you got noting and you vanting some nice dress to catch the man. I give to you von hundred dollar to clean my birdcage.

CATHERINE: No.

> ANA *takes out a hundred dollars. She tries to hand it to* CATHERINE.

ANA: Please. Take it. You killing me.

CATHERINE: Don't be silly, Ana.

ANA: You don't vant my money?

CATHERINE: No.

ANA: But everyvone vant my money. Is for this I is hiding. Many people vant to kill me for the money. They tink, rich old lady who never got the childer—

CATHERINE: You never had children?

ANA: Don't be sticky nose, Kitty-kitty. Must to clean the birdcage. Then ve talking. Is your payment instead of the hundred dollar. But must to clean good.

SCENE FIVE

KEN *is on the computer, playing World of Warcraft.* CATHERINE *comes out and stands before him. She is dressed nicely.*

CATHERINE: How does this look?

KEN: Great! My aunt is excited about meeting you. I told her she's just setting herself up for disappointment, of course.

CATHERINE: Of course.

KEN: Seriously, you look great.

CATHERINE: Thanks, Ken. This was nice of you.

KEN: Ironic, isn't it? That I should do something nice for you when I hate you so much. Anything to keep you from bringing more Tupperware into the house.

CATHERINE: See you later.

KEN: Later.

> *As she's walking out he calls out, really meaning it:*

Good luck!

SCENE SIX

CATHERINE *walks out onto the street. Her telephone rings. She holds it in her hand, not answering. It stops. On the street, there is* ANA.

CATHERINE: Hello, Ana!

ANA: Kitty-kitty! I glad I see you. You got the time?

CATHERINE: It's half past twelve.

ANA: No, I mean, you, got, the, time?

CATHERINE: What time?

ANA: You got time for helping me leetle bit?

CATHERINE: I've got a job interview.

ANA: Vhat time?

CATHERINE: Three o'clock.

ANA: You got two and a half hours.

CATHERINE: It's on the other side of town.

ANA: Vhy you vorking so far? I give you the job. Only across the Mary Street. You got the time to come to chemist vith me?

> CATHERINE *thinks about this.*

CATHERINE: I don't know.

ANA: You is catching the bus?

CATHERINE: Yes.

ANA: Chemist is next to the bus.

CATHERINE: Okay.

ANA: Good girl.

SCENE SEVEN

ANA *and* CATHERINE *go into the chemist shop together. The young* CHEMIST *from before is working there. He looks up happily when he sees* ANA *and* CATHERINE.

CHEMIST: Hello, Mrs Brajavik.

ANA: Hello.

CHEMIST: Who's your sidekick?

ANA: This is the Kitty-kitty. She is the neighbour.

> The CHEMIST *is warm towards* CATHERINE.

CHEMIST: That's nice that you're hanging out with Ana.

CATHERINE: Oh, thanks. It's nice that she's hanging out with me.

CHEMIST: Do you live on Mary Street too?

CATHERINE: Yes—

> ANA *stage whispers out the side of her mouth to* CATHERINE.

ANA: Shht! Don't jump.

CATHERINE: I live nearby. Do you?

CHEMIST: I live in Box Hill.

ANA: Ja, very good the Box Hill. Like Europe. Very Europe the Box Hill. Vhat you find there, you got novhere. Novhere in the Austral!

CHEMIST: Here's your refill, Mrs Brajavik.

ANA: Tank you. Tank you.

CHEMIST: It's nice to meet you, Kitty-kitty.

CATHERINE: It's actually—

> ANA *hisses out the side of her mouth again.*

ANA: Don't jump!

CATHERINE: Nice to meet you too.

> ANA *and* CATHERINE *walk back out onto the street.*

ANA: He is the very good boy.

CATHERINE: Yes.

ANA: Very intellygent. Eyes like computer.

CATHERINE: Yes.

ANA: You should to marry von such a man.

CATHERINE: Ana!

ANA: Oh, yes! You vill be lucky if he take you. Never tell him you live vith the man as friend. No-von should to know. Don't con-fess. Final. Yes, my sveetheart. Only yesterday I am tinking of you vhen I am vatching the 'Doctor Phil'. Many tings you be learning from him. Many tings. Oh, the stupid girl who chase the man. He leave her for her sister. And she cry and cry and say, 'I just vant him back!' But he no vant to come! Ja. She is the stupid. Like you.

CATHERINE: Ana, you don't know me. I'm not stupid.

ANA: No—not your fault! No, no, no! It is the nature. Is the nature making you stupid. You got the good nature. Too good. Should to learn to see the trouble. Like Ana. Come. I teaching you.

> *They walk back towards Ana's house.* CATHERINE *seems to have forgotten she was catching the bus.*

SCENE EIGHT

Inside Ana's house. They have made Hungarian doughnuts. ANA *is eating one.*

ANA: Very special. Very good. Ve make the very good Hungarian doughnut. Vhy you no eating?

CATHERINE: I'm not hungry.

ANA: No! Must to eat. Must to!

> ANA *holds out some doughnuts to* CATHERINE. CATHERINE *is very nervous about eating doughnuts. But she picks a little piece off one and puts it in her mouth.*

CATHERINE: Delicious.

ANA: Now vhen the Doctor Vhite come, you must to tell her that you— you are for the doughnuts. You. She should not to know. Vhat business of hers if I should to eat someting? They are for you. You has made them for the boy you live vith.

CATHERINE: But he's diabetic.

ANA: Shh-shh-shh! The Vhite don't know dat.

The doorbell rings.

She is here! Quickly! Quickly!

ANA *races to the door. She opens it. There is* JOVANKA, *smiling pleasantly at* ANA.

JOVANKA: Hello, Ana. I come for one coffee.

ANA: Jovanka. You is not the Vhite.

JOVANKA: You want one coffee?

ANA: I don't got the time.

She shuts the door in JOVANKA's *face.*

Vhy the Vhite alvays late?

CATHERINE: I'm sure she'll come if you have an appointment.

ANA: You is the naïve girl. She is no the doctor I can trust on, the Vhite.

CATHERINE: Maybe you should change doctors.

ANA: I cannot. Because the Vhite vas my husband doctor. She is the pretty voman, but she is the secret vasp. You know who she look like?

CATHERINE: Who?

ANA: The Palin. She look like the Sarah Palin. And both of as intellygent as the other. Ja, I have known many Vhites. In the camps, many Vhites.

CATHERINE: What camps?

ANA: Vhen I is in detention. Many people. Like to keep the powers over Ana. Pushing me down vith the rules. Never mind. I fix her. Ana vill be all the time vinner.

CATHERINE: I don't think you should be in competition with your doctor, Ana.

ANA: No, is no competition. Is the var. You understand noting. You have never been for the vorld. You is never even marry. You should to love this boy you live vith. Is it because he is the de-a-bet-ic? You don't vant the sick boy? Better you is marry the Ken.

CATHERINE: But I don't want to marry the Ken.

ANA: Ana is like you. Live vith the man who vas not my husband—and he lock me!

CATHERINE: Lost you?

ANA: No! No! He lock me! In the rooms. No tea. No milk. No von biscuit. He lock me! Every night. Very dangerous.

CATHERINE: What did he do to you?

ANA: Is terrible. Vas very terrible for Ana. I am the young voman. He don't speak the Hungary. I don't speak the English. But both of us speak the Italiano.

CATHERINE: When was this?

ANA: Vhen I first arrive to the Austral I got noting. Noting. No von cent. No friend. No family. No good clothings. But I is still very glamour. That's Ana. I get the job vith the very big Catholic doctor. I nursing his dying vife. Then she is dead, and he keep me still. He vhisper—he pray—in the Italiano outside my bedroom all through the nights. I is frighten.

CATHERINE: What did he do?

ANA: Nothing. Nothing. Dis vas the problem. He no vant to make the sex. Only to lock me.

CATHERINE: Was he your boyfriend?

ANA: No! No! My bossy. Like the Ken.

CATHERINE: Ken's not my bossy.

ANA: My bossy vas very big Catholic. Very big. Too much Catholic to use the sausage.

CATHERINE: Catholics can't eat sausage?

ANA: Vhy you so stupid? The sausage. The sausage of the man.

CATHERINE: You wanted him to use his sausage?

ANA: I am no sure. Sometimes my mind vanting von ting, the heart vanting the other. And the sausage and pussy cat vant tings all their own. My pussy cat don't know vhat she vant. But my mind do not like Ana to be locked anymore in the room.

CATHERINE: How did you escape?

ANA: I go secretly early morning and get the new job. Vith the nuns. Alvays the Catholic bugger. The Catholic ruin Ana many time. Vhen I go home, he is vaiting for me. He know. He know that I vill be going. He take me, for first time, he take me drive in his car. Ve are not talking. He drive only short distance and then back onto his street. And then he say in the Italiano, 'Ana street'. And then he say to me, 'Ana car'. And then he stop at his home. And he say, 'Ana house'. I say, back on the Italiano, 'No. Not Ana's.' And he say, 'Solo una Ana. Solo una Ana.' And I say back on him, 'No. Many Ana. Everyvhere Ana.' He crying now. And he say, 'Solo una Ana. Solo una Ana.' And he is right. Only von Ana. And that night, Ana lock her own door. And in the morning, she is going.

ANA *is back from the story. She looks at* CATHERINE.

You see. Very complicated to live vith the man who is not the husband. If there is no the sex, you is the prisoner. [*She considers this.*] And sometime vith the sex you is the prisoner too.

SCENE NINE

CATHERINE *gets home.* KEN *is sitting in front of the computer screen.* CATHERINE *is carrying their mail.* KEN *is eating jellybeans. He doesn't look up at* CATHERINE.

KEN: Hey.
CATHERINE: Hi.

> *He still doesn't really look at her.*

What's wrong? Are you having a hypo?
KEN: Just a little one. I'll be okay in a sec.
CATHERINE: You okay?
KEN: Yeah, yeah. I said I'll be okay in a sec.

> CATHERINE *watches him. He checks his insulin levels.*

Back on track.

> *He looks at the mail in her hand.*

Any interesting mail?
CATHERINE: Only bills.
KEN: Don't worry, no-one expects payment during recession.
CATHERINE: That's a relief. Pretty generous of the gas company.
KEN: Everyone does their bit.

> CATHERINE *senses* KEN *is being distant.*

CATHERINE: Did you hear back from your producer?
KEN: Nobody does anything they say they're going to do in this country.
CATHERINE: Then fire them.
KEN: I can't fire them when I don't pay them.
CATHERINE: Killed any monsters?
KEN: As a matter of fact, I'm in the middle of a raid right now. How come you didn't go to your job interview?

> *The realisation that she forgot hits* CATHERINE.

CATHERINE: Shit.

KEN: You actually forgot?

CATHERINE: I'm sorry.

KEN: My aunt called me. They waited for you all afternoon. How could you forget, Catherine? You left here to go to the interview. What happened?

CATHERINE: I got busy.

KEN: Doing what?

CATHERINE: Talking to a neighbour.

KEN: Talking to a neighbour? Which one?

CATHERINE: How many of our neighbours do you know?

KEN: None of them.

CATHERINE: If I described one of them, would you know which one I meant?

KEN: No.

CATHERINE: Then why do you ask which one?

KEN: Alright, who is it? Tell me about our neighbour.

CATHERINE: Why do you always need to know where I am?

KEN: I'm just wondering which neighbour was so important to talk to that you missed the interview I set up for you.

CATHERINE: I said I'm sorry.

KEN: I think I liked you better when you used to eat.

CATHERINE: I eat all the time.

KEN: Yeah, you eat carrots all the time. Do you know you're actually starting to turn orange?

CATHERINE: No I'm not.

KEN: Your hands are orange.

CATHERINE: It's my natural skin tone.

KEN: You look like a 'Simpsons' character.

CATHERINE: You're just being mean.

KEN: You weren't really with a neighbour, were you?

CATHERINE: You think I would lie?

KEN: I'm sorry. But it is strange, Catherine.

CATHERINE: Why are you so concerned about where I am?

KEN: Because I'm your friend.

CATHERINE: I don't think that's it.

KEN: What else would it be, Cathy?

CATHERINE: Don't call me that.

Being called Cathy has upset her. She turns away, trying to hide this. But KEN *can see.*

KEN: Do you wanna start over?

CATHERINE: What do you mean?

KEN: Start the whole thing over. You come back in the door, and say:

CATHERINE: Hey.

KEN: Hey, Catherine.

CATHERINE: Are you having a hypo?

KEN: Just a little one. I'll be okay in a sec. [*He checks his insulin levels.*] Back on track. You wanna watch an ep?

CATHERINE: Okay.

    Catherine's phone begins to ring and ring. She doesn't answer.

SCENE TEN

ANA *answers the door to* CATHERINE. *Inside Ana's house, the telephone is ringing.* ANA *looks at* CATHERINE.

ANA: Ansver dat.

CATHERINE: What do I say?

ANA: Nothing! You say nothing!

    CATHERINE *looks confused, but answers the phone.*

CATHERINE: Hello, Ana's house. [*She listens.*] Hello, Jovanka.

    ANA *starts giving her frantic 'No! No! No!' motions. But it is too late.*

Uh yes, Ana's right here.

    ANA *takes the phone and speaks icily to* JOVANKA.

ANA: Hello, Jovanka. I cannot speak. I am very busy. I have the visitor. No. No coffee. Goodbye. [*She looks at* CATHERINE.] Vhy you answer dat phone?

CATHERINE: Because you told me to.

ANA: But I never tell you to tell the Jovanka I is here. You should to be more smart behaving.

CATHERINE: But what was I meant to say to her?

ANA: Nothing. You should to have said nothing.

CATHERINE: But then what's the point in answering the phone?

ANA: Ja, Ana is teaching you. Kitty-kitty I am in the bad. I feel it vith my ultrasound.

CATHERINE: Ultrasound?

ANA: Like the x-ray, but more feely. It is the sixth sense. Alvays tell Ana vhen she is in the bad. It all the time tell me vhen coming someting sad. For example, vhen it vas var in Hungary. I live in the house vith my mummy, my daddy, two sister and my brother. And von night, the gypsy come to sing beneath our vindow. Everyvone know that vhen gypsy come to sing, he have been sent by von young man to sing love song to the girl he love.

A GYPSY *begins to sing beneath the window. In Hungarian.*

The lounge room shifts slightly into Hungary. CATHERINE *feels it, sees it, she is half in the lounge room, half in Hungary watching* ANA, *who suddenly seems younger. Like a young girl.*

My daddy is angry on me. He say:

ANA'S FATHER *appears in Hungary.*

FATHER: Ana, you did not tell me there is young man who love you.

YOUNG ANA: There isn't. Not von, Daddy. [*She looks back to* CATHERINE.] My daddy don't believe me. But I know no young man love me. And I feel it. Strong vith my sixth sense. I feel the gypsy is singing for my daddy. Not me. But for him.

FATHER: The gypsy don't never get sent to sing love song for old man! Only for the young girl.

CATHERINE *asks across the lounge room, her voice reaching into Hungary:*

CATHERINE: Ana? What are the words to the song? In English?

The GYPSY *changes from singing in Hungarian to singing in English.*

GYPSY: [*sung*]
Never anymore vill the star to shining in the sky above this roof,
All the vindows on this street are open,
But von vhich is close,
Never to open,

Never anymore vill the flowers grow beneath this vindow,
Von person I love from this house has gone,
Never to come,
Never, never anymore.

CATHERINE: That's a love song?

ANA: In the Hungary, yes. And coming the next day…

ANA, *as a young woman, watches her parents arguing.*

FATHER: I am not going to the vork today.

MOTHER: You must to.

FATHER: I am the tire. I vant to stay. I stay home vith you and the childer. Just von day. Just today, I am at home vith you and the childer.

MOTHER: The childer is starving. Not today for the lazy. You must to go to the vork. Or ve is all dying. Ve got no food. Nothing. And you vant to staying home. You must to be the good father.

FATHER: I am the good father. I just no vant to go. Von day. Just von day, I vant to stay home.

MOTHER: Vhy? Vhy?

FATHER: I just vant to. In my stomachs.

MOTHER: Vhy I marry the lazy man? Who no care his family starving? Cold? Vhy I should to marry?

FATHER: I go. I go.

ANA'S FATHER *storms out.*

ANA: And the day passing. A knock come on the door. My sixth sense tell me vhat it vill be.

ANA'S SISTER *hears the knock too.*

SISTER: I get Mummy.

YOUNG ANA: No. Don't get Mummy. Ve ansver.

ANA *opens the door. There is a* SOLDIER *there. When* ANA *and her* SISTER *stand before him, he takes his hat off.*

SOLDIER: Hello. Your mummy is home?

ANA: [*young*] No. My mummy not home. Vhat has happen?

[*Back in the present*] And the soldier he tell me. Going to the vork, bomb coming. My daddy was blown to pieces in the street. Killed. After officer go, I take my sisters into the toilet and say, 'Don't tell Mummy. Don't tell Mummy. She vill be too sad. Don't tell Mummy.'

So ve hide in the toilet to cry. And don't tell. Not for whole day. My brother in army, he go to pick up the pieces of our daddy on the street. Ana go vith him. And after all is picked up, then ve tell Mummy. You see, Ana knew. The ultrasound. Dat song vas for my daddy.

> ANA *begins to sing the song. In English. The* GYPSY *joins her. And* ANA'S FATHER, *back in Hungary, all that time ago.*

ANA, GYPSY, ANA'S FATHER: [*sung, together*]
> Never anymore vill the star to shining in the sky above this roof,
> All the vindows on this street are open,
> But von vhich is close,
> Never to open,
> Never anymore vill the flower grow beneath this vindow,
> Von person I love from this house has gone,
> Never to come,
> Never, never anymore.

CATHERINE: Never anymore.

> CATHERINE *looks at* ANA, *as Hungary swirls around them, and then disappears.*

SCENE ELEVEN

CATHERINE *arrives home. The house is in that semi-darkness with a tinge of blue that occurs when there's no light but for the television and computer screens.*

KEN *has fallen asleep in front of his laptop. A 'West Wing' episode has ended on DVD, and now just theme music on the DVD options is playing over and over again. The house is a mess.* KEN *has left plates and cups all around.* CATHERINE *begins to clean up. She wipes the table. She is softly singing the 'Never Anymore' song to herself while she does it.* KEN *does not wake up.*

Her phone rings. CATHERINE *stops singing. She thinks about it. She holds it in her hand ringing, finishes the song. And then she answers.*

CATHERINE: Hello.

> *She stands there with the phone to her ear. The whole world is different now.*

SCENE TWELVE

CATHERINE *steps outside. There's no-one there.*

CATHERINE: Hello?

> *No answer.*

> *She looks around, half relieved, half bitterly disappointed. She turns to go. And then a young man steps out.* MARTIN.

MARTIN: Hey, Cathy.

> *She lets him call her Cathy—it seems as though this is his usual nickname for her.*

CATHERINE: Hey.

MARTIN: Long time no see.

CATHERINE: Two years.

MARTIN: Is it that long?

CATHERINE: Lost track of time, have you?

MARTIN: A little bit. You know me.

CATHERINE: Not really.

MARTIN: You do, Cathy.

CATHERINE: Why have you been calling me?

MARTIN: For the same reason that you answered. Because I miss you. All the time.

CATHERINE: I'm finally getting my life together. Since you left.

MARTIN: I'm so glad to hear that.

CATHERINE: Are you?

MARTIN: Of course. You must know I want what's best for you.

CATHERINE: Then why are you here?

MARTIN: Cathy, I promise you—I'm getting my life together too.

CATHERINE: Don't say that.

MARTIN: This time is different. I know that sounds like a cliché, Cathy. But this time I'm going to make it work. With you.

CATHERINE: I'm so angry at you…

MARTIN: I know. [*He takes a step towards her.*] How about how you look exactly the same? How about how you haven't aged since the day I met you?

CATHERINE: Neither have you.

MARTIN: Maybe neither of us age while we're away from the other one. That's kinda cool. But kinda sad too. Like time doesn't count when we're not together.

CATHERINE: I've felt like that. I've felt like I've fallen out of time since you left.

MARTIN: I still want you. My whole body, Cathy. My whole body still wants you.

CATHERINE: Don't say that.

MARTIN: It's true. Look at me.

CATHERINE: It always ends the same.

MARTIN: Not this time. Look at me, Cathy. Not this time. This time it can end however you want it to.

CATHERINE: But—why does it have to end at all?

MARTIN: It doesn't.

CATHERINE: You should go. I've got ironing to do. And I'm in the middle of cleaning the cupboards.

MARTIN: That's what you said when we first met. Do you remember? You said you couldn't go out with me that night because you had to go home and iron. Remember?

CATHERINE: Yes.

MARTIN: That was so cute. But then you came anyway. Remember?

CATHERINE: Yes.

MARTIN: We went out to dinner and you ordered exactly the same meal as me.

CATHERINE: I get ordering anxiety.

MARTIN: And then you teased me about my cologne. But I wasn't wearing any. It's just the way I smell.

CATHERINE: You smelled like the pews in a church. You smelled like wood. Do you smell like that now?

MARTIN: Smell me.

CATHERINE: I'm scared.

MARTIN: Come here. Smell me, Cathy.

She doesn't move. He speaks softly.

Come here.

She walks and stands in front of him.

No. Here.

He stands right up close to her, almost touching.

She breathes in deep.

CATHERINE: Yes. The same. You smell exactly the same.

MARTIN: Give me a chance.

CATHERINE: I can't. I promised myself.

MARTIN: Please. One more chance.

SCENE THIRTEEN

ANA *sits in the Neighbourhood Watch meeting, amongst other neighbours. She is looking around for* CATHERINE. *A* POLICEMAN *is standing up before the group, speaking. He is fairly young.*

CATHERINE *slips quietly into the meeting, and makes her way to sit down next to* ANA. ANA *speaks to* CATHERINE *as the* POLICEMAN *speaks.*

ANA: You is late.

CATHERINE: Sorry.

ANA: Very bad. The lateness very bad. You vas rude to the police gentlyman by being the late.

CATHERINE: Sorry, Ana.

ANA: Good.

She watches the POLICEMAN *speaking.*

He is the young. Like you.

CATHERINE: Yes.

ANA: Everyvone else the old bastard. Must to be he is your boyfriend.

CATHERINE: Ana!

ANA: You no like the police gentlyman? Very dignity. Ja, should to be in the luck if the police gentlyman your boyfriend!

POLICEMAN: Thanks very much for having me here to speak to you this evening. I just wanted to start off by saying that already, just by attending a Neighbourhood Watch meeting, you're making my job easier. By knowing your neighbourhood, by being a part of your community, you are the best ones to spot signs of trouble, and you can keep each other informed. A close community is the best way to make sure that individuals stay safe. If we know our neighbours, we can look after our neighbours. And if we look after our neighbours, then our neighbours can look after us. The best way to fight crime is to prevent it from happening in the first place. Now the first step to a safe street is to be familiar—

ANA *interrupts in a sweet, polite voice.*

ANA: Excuse me, Mr Police Gentlyman. May I to ask you von question?

POLICEMAN: Um, certainly, ma'am. Did you want to ask it now or in question time at the end?

ANA: Better now. If I am valking on the street. On the Mary Street. Vith my dog Bella. Who is the German Shepherd vith leetle, leetle bit the Doberman Pincher. But on the leads—alvays on the leads—I never for no von moment take my Bella off the leads.

POLICEMAN: That's good.

ANA: So I am no breaking any law?

POLICEMAN: Not so far.

ANA: And I valking the Bella on her lead and coming down the street von lady and vith her von leetle, vhite Piccolo. And this Piccolo is no on the leads. Is this lady breaking any laws?

POLICEMAN: She should have her dog on the lead in a residential area.

ANA: And I catch it—I see—I know the animal—and I know that leetle Piccolo vill be running on my Bella. I scream on the lady—'Put your dog on the lead! Put your dog on the lead!' I scream on her. But she listen too late. And already vhite Piccolo running, jumping on my Bella.

POLICEMAN: It sounds like the Piccolo had a suicide wish!

ANA: Ja! Crazy! He jump on the Bella! And my Bella put leetle Piccolo in her mouth and shake like rags. Lady scream on me—but alvays my Bella vas on the lead. Bella drop the Piccolo and lady pick up in her arms and run. Now I ask you, Mr Police Gentlyman. Is my Bella in the bad?

POLICEMAN: No, you did the right thing. Your dog was on the lead.

ANA: You vill not be coming to put von bullet in my Bella?

He laughs.

POLICEMAN: No. I won't be coming to shoot your dog, ma'am.

ANA: Tank you! Tank you!

POLICEMAN: Have I answered your question?

ANA: Oh, yes—very much the ansver! Very much!

As the POLICEMAN *continues to talk to the meeting,* ANA *stage whispers to* CATHERINE. *Everyone can hear her.*

POLICEMAN: / By paying attention to what your street looks like normally, to the people who are usually on your street/

ANA: / You hear that? I ask him—Is my Bella in the bad?—and he say, 'No!' He say Piccolo vas the suicide—Piccolo broke the law!

POLICEMAN: / To the cars that are usually parked on your street—you can tell when something is different or suspicious. Now I'm not saying that you should be paranoid—because that doesn't help anyone. I'm just saying that the first step to safety, is being aware/

ANA: / I ask the police gentlyman—your boyfriend—have I broken the laws? And he say, 'No!' You see the Jovanka spying from her vindow vant to put me in the bad. But now I got the proof. You are learning from Ana, Kitty-kitty?

The end of the Neighbourhood Watch meeting. KATRINA *is passing by* ANA. ANA *spots her.*

Katrina! You hear, I make the very big question on the police gentlyman.

KATRINA: I heard.

ANA: He says I am not in the bad.

KATRINA: Well, it certainly sounds like things will be fine. [*She turns to* CATHERINE.] Hello, my name's Katrina.

ANA: This is the Kitty-kitty.

KATRINA: You live on Mary Street, don't you?

CATHERINE: Yes.

KATRINA: I've hardly seen you there. Strange. I suppose now, we'll run into each other all the time. That's how it works, isn't it? Once someone comes into your life, they stay there.

ANA: Not alvays.

KATRINA: That's a good point, Ana. I don't know what I was saying. Most times people are gone before you can remember their name. Ha ha. I'm not good with names. I've never been. And now I'm worse.

ANA *speaks to* CATHERINE.

ANA: Katrina got the very nice house, Kitty-kitty.

KATRINA: Thank you, Ana.

ANA: She got the many television.

KATRINA: They're security screens. I've got cameras all around the outside of my house and in the spare bedroom. And they can see in the dark, these cameras. So I always know if I'm safe.

ANA: They go everyvhere?

KATRINA: Everywhere.

ANA: I like very much these camera and television. But I don't need, I got the Bella. She all ting. My daughter, my security camera and my veapon. Tell me, Katrina, you got the two childer. The grown daughter and son. You don't vant von of them live here vith you?

KATRINA: No!

ANA: You don't get lonely?

KATRINA: I'm alone. But I'm never lonely. I like it this way. It certainly beats when I was married. [*She smiles at* CATHERINE.] Never listen to older women talk about their husbands, Kitty-kitty. You'll never get married.

ANA: She is not for the husband.

CATHERINE: I'm not?

ANA: Ana know. She like her freedom. Too much.

They begin to walk home together.

KATRINA: Keep your freedom, Kitty-kitty. It's so nice. My time is all my own now. Would you like to see what I'm making?

CATHERINE: Sorry?

KATRINA *takes from her bag a small, knitted doll wearing a dress that is half-made. She takes another couple of doll dresses and hands them to* CATHERINE, *and then, as an afterthought, for* ANA *too, to have a look at.*

KATRINA: I make these for charity. They give them to the children.

CATHERINE: How nice.

ANA: These dresses, someting very special.

KATRINA: I used to make more. But I get so tired now with the chemo.

CATHERINE: You're getting chemo?

KATRINA: Oh, yes.

ANA: Don't be sticky nose, Kitty.

CATHERINE: You look so well. And you have all your hair—

KATRINA *laughs.*

KATRINA: Thank you, Kitty. But you know this is a wig.

CATHERINE: I didn't. I didn't know.

ANA: My husband had the cancers. Died. Poor tings.

KATRINA: Yes. Well, thanks for walking me home, ladies.

KATRINA *goes to walk into her drive, but then stops suddenly. Frozen.*

ANA: Vhat? Vhat you see?

KATRINA: I thought I saw something.

ANA: Von man?

KATRINA: Yes. For a moment I thought it was a man. Outside that house.

ANA: The Kitty's house. I get the Bella.

KATRINA: No. No, that's not necessary, Ana. My eyes make mistakes now—especially in the dark.

ANA: Better I get the Bella. Ve all going into the home, checking everyting for safety.

KATRINA: I'm sorry, I just need to go to bed. I just need to go to bed.

ANA: Remember police gentlyman said if ve see anyting unusual—

KATRINA: Goodnight, Ana. Nice to meet you, Kitty.

KATRINA *is making her way back to her house.*

CATHERINE: Next time, to the next meeting we'll bring Hungarian doughnuts. Ana makes them. I'm her assistant.

KATRINA: Well, that sounds lovely. Goodnight, ladies.

CATHERINE: Goodnight!

ANA *says nothing.* KATRINA *goes inside. It is just* ANA *and* CATHERINE *now.*

ANA: You know vhat you done wrong?

CATHERINE: No.

ANA: Don't be the baby horse.

CATHERINE: The baby horse?

ANA: The baby horse all the time try to run in front of the mummy horse. But is stupid. Go wrong vay.

CATHERINE: When? What did I do?

ANA: Vonce you jump is too late. Cannot to go back.

CATHERINE: When did I jump? When was I the baby horse?

ANA: Tink. Use your brain.

CATHERINE: What?

ANA: The doughnuts.

CATHERINE: The doughnuts?

ANA: You should never to say ve make the doughnut. If come next Neighbourhood Vatch meeting and ve make, then ve make. Surprise. But ve

don't know. Ve don't know vhat happen before then. And now ve have
the responsibility.

CATHERINE: I'm sure no-one will mind if we don't make—

ANA: Ve vill be in the shame. Better not to jump. Don't be the baby horse.

CATHERINE: Okay. I won't be the baby horse.

ANA: You vant I getting the Bella? Check your house?

CATHERINE: It's okay, Ken's there.

ANA: Good. Vhy you late tonight? You is vith the man?

CATHERINE: Yes.

ANA: You make the sex vith this man. Tell me the truth. I know if you
lying me.

CATHERINE: No.

ANA: You lying me.

CATHERINE: I swear we didn't make the sex.

ANA: He try?

CATHERINE: No.

ANA: Sure?

CATHERINE: Sure.

ANA: Vhat is wrong vith this man? You try?

CATHERINE: No!

ANA: Good. Never hang off the man. 'Bye 'bye, Austral pie.

CATHERINE: 'Bye 'bye, Hungarian pie.

They part.

SCENE FOURTEEN

CATHERINE *comes into the house.* KEN *is there. He is playing World of
Warcraft.*

KEN: Where have you been? That's right. I'm not meant to ask.

CATHERINE: It's okay. I've been at the Neighbourhood Watch meeting.

KEN: What? No you haven't.

CATHERINE: It was really interesting.

KEN: You mean to tell me you really, actually went to a Neighbourhood
Watch meeting?

CATHERINE: Yeah.

KEN: Why?

CATHERINE: You know, if we all knew our neighbours, our neighbourhoods
would be real communities.

KEN: Who are you? Do you know why people move to the city?

CATHERINE: Why?

KEN: Because in small towns everyone knows everything about everyone else. And everyone minds everyone else's business.

CATHERINE: What business do you have that you want to hide from the neighbours?

KEN: Lots of stuff.

CATHERINE: Like what? I mean, is it really so terrible if they know you just sit here at the table and play World of Warcraft? I mean, what are they going to see, you hardly even leave the house.

KEN: You're being pretty uppity for someone who's been to just one Neighbourhood Watch meeting. I don't know if you can really talk as though you're 'Miss Involved with the World'. And I don't have to justify myself to you—but I'm going to. World of Warcraft is a community. It's a global community. Tonight I went on a raid with members of my guild—one is a housewife from Toronto, one is a high school student from Wales, one is a computer programmer from Miami, Cathy—

CATHERINE: Catherine.

KEN: Catherine. The point is, World of Warcraft introduces me to people I normally have no access to in life. And I get to know them.

CATHERINE: Listen to yourself. You just said people who you have no access to in life. This isn't life. Just sitting at the table, looking into that screen.

KEN: Catherine, stop picking fights with me.

CATHERINE: I have to be honest.

KEN: If we were both honest about one another's lives, I don't know if we could be friends.

CATHERINE: What do you mean?

KEN: Don't ask.

CATHERINE: What?

KEN: Don't ask unless you're ready to hear the truth. Because once I say it, I can't take it back.

> CATHERINE *looks ill at ease for a moment. She realises she doesn't want to hear it.*

CATHERINE: Okay. Don't then.

> *But* KEN *says it anyway.*

KEN: You have to get over him.

CATHERINE: I said don't say it.

KEN: You do. You have to get over Martin.

CATHERINE: You don't know anything about me.

KEN: I know everything about you. I'm like your Neighbourhood Watch.

CATHERINE: Well, stop watching.

KEN: I can't. It's my job.

CATHERINE: It's not your goddamn job. Leave me alone.

KEN: Catherine—

CATHERINE: Get fucked.

KEN: Did you just tell me to get fucked?

CATHERINE: Get fucked! Get fucked!

> CATHERINE *leaves.*

> KEN *sits by himself. In front of his laptop.*

KEN: I need a minute to think about that. That was quite full-on. I just need to be on my own for a bit, actually.

SCENE FIFTEEN

CATHERINE *runs out into the street.* MARTIN *is there.*

MARTIN: Cathy.

CATHERINE: What are you doing here?

MARTIN: Ken really hates me, huh?

CATHERINE: Martin!

MARTIN: I came over to ask you something.

CATHERINE: What?

MARTIN: Will you come on a picnic with me?

CATHERINE: It's too late.

MARTIN: It's a night picnic.

CATHERINE: Martin…

MARTIN: Please? If you say no, then I'll have to have one by myself and that will be so depressing.

CATHERINE: Where?

MARTIN: Here in the dark woods. Your favourite place.

CATHERINE: I don't play The Woods anymore.

MARTIN: That's a shame. Because I brought your favourite trail mix.

CATHERINE: I don't like trail mix anymore.

MARTIN: Wow. You used to eat the whole bag in the first two minutes.

CATHERINE: See, I've changed. [*She thinks for a moment.*] Does it have chocolate chips in it?

MARTIN: Yup.

He pulls out a little bag. And holds it before her.

CATHERINE: There'll be bears.

MARTIN: It's okay, I'm armed. I've brought honey. Honey always stops bears right in their tracks.

CATHERINE: But I want to eat the honey.

MARTIN: You want everything! You can have one spoonful.

He lays out a picnic blanket. He sits on the blanket and pats beside him, motioning for CATHERINE *to sit next to him. She hesitates, and then does.* MARTIN *lays out picnic items.*

One Quiche Lorraine. One thermos of French onion soup. That's just for starters.

They sit beside each other silently. Not eating.

Is it because of me you're not eating?

CATHERINE: I am eating.

CATHERINE *looks down.*

MARTIN: I adore you.

CATHERINE: Shut up.

MARTIN: Have you been seeing anyone? Since me?

CATHERINE: No.

MARTIN: At all?

CATHERINE: Two dates. But they were weird.

MARTIN: What was weird?

CATHERINE: It made me think about you.

MARTIN: Good. What about Ken? How is he?

CATHERINE: Fine. He's still waiting to make his film.

MARTIN: Still?

CATHERINE: It seems to take a while.

MARTIN: Tell me what else. Tell me what's been going on in your life.

CATHERINE: Not all that much. I moved into this house. I quit four jobs. I was fired from one.

MARTIN: Have you been doing any acting?

CATHERINE: No. I did a voice and movement workshop.

MARTIN: Show me what you learned.

CATHERINE: No!

MARTIN: Please!

CATHERINE: I'll just do one line for you—that's all.

> *She thinks for a moment. She stands up, and begins a movement with it:*

> *Out, damn'd spot! out, I say!—One; two: why, then 'tis time to do 't.— Hell is murky.—Fie, my lord, fie, a soldier, and afeard?*

> *He laughs. She does too.*

MARTIN: What else? Tell me what else.

CATHERINE: I have a new friend. Her name is Ana and she lives across the street. She's Hungarian.

MARTIN: I think I saw her. Earlier.

CATHERINE: When?

MARTIN: When I was on your doorstep. She's got a big dog?

CATHERINE: Yeah.

MARTIN: And she's your new friend.

CATHERINE: Yeah.

MARTIN: Perfect.

> *He touches her hair.*

You're still cutting your own hair.

CATHERINE: Does it look really bad?

MARTIN: Beautiful.

CATHERINE: Why did you leave?

MARTIN: Don't ask that.

CATHERINE: Tell me what I did.

MARTIN: Nothing. Cathy. Nothing. [*He looks up at the sky.*] Hey, look up. Bats.

> *His phone beeps with a text message. He takes the phone out.*

CATHERINE: You've still got your old phone.

> *He reads the text message.*

MARTIN: Shit. Cathy, I'm so sorry, I'm gonna have to run.

CATHERINE: But we just got here.

MARTIN: I completely forgot. I was meant to be meet someone.

CATHERINE: Maybe we can meet later?

MARTIN: Sorry, this is gonna take a while.

CATHERINE: Oh.

MARTIN: Next time we'll stay here all night. Promise. Hey, you keep the food, in case you want a snack later.

CATHERINE: I don't want it—

He gets up to leave, then turns back around.

MARTIN: Want me to walk you home?

CATHERINE: I'm going to stay here.

MARTIN: I'm sorry about this, Cathy. I'll make it up to you. Next time. Catch you soon.

He leaves.

SCENE SIXTEEN

CATHERINE *arrives in Ana's house.* ANA *looks her over.*

ANA: You has been chasing the man.

CATHERINE: No I haven't.

ANA: Don't lying me. I can no help you if you is lying me. You chase? And he no vant you?

CATHERINE: It's complicated.

ANA: He don't vant. Tell the truth and I know if you lying me, this boy you love, you make the sex with him?

CATHERINE: No. He was just interested in the quiche he made for the picnic.

ANA: Oh, my sveetheart. My poor sveetheart. Oh, how you is the stupid. This boy you love—vith the quiche. He is the secret homosexual! Ja, it is the vay. All the time vith the quiche. Very softly and nice, but never the sausage for you. Even in the picnic! You is the attractive young girl. Good legs. He should to be pushing you onto the blanket! Don't be sad, no, no, no. Better you is know.

CATHERINE: Will you tell me another story, Ana?

ANA: First I like to testing someting. Take off your shoes. I like to veighing you.

CATHERINE: Let's not…

ANA: Take. Off. Your. Shoes.

CATHERINE *reluctantly takes off her shoes.* ANA *points her towards the scale.*

Stand on.

> CATHERINE *steps onto the scale. Even though it is daylight,* ANA *leans down with a very small torch and looks into the scale.*

Ja. Should to go up leetle bit.

CATHERINE: Really?

ANA: Ja, vhen I vas young I vas all the time skinny, but not too skinny. Not the skinny of the crazy. You vant story, you must to eat the chicken in my frigider.

CATHERINE: That whole chicken?

ANA: Okay, half of. Half for you. Half for me. Deal or no deal?

CATHERINE: Deal.

ANA: Final. Now I tell…

> *Just then, a knock on the door.*

Who coming now?

> *She stalks up to the door. She calls out suspiciously and cautiously.*

Hello?

> *A* VOICE *answers back.*

VOICE: Hello? Ana?

> ANA *opens the door and there is* JOVANKA.

ANA: Oh. It is you. Jovanka.

JOVANKA: We was worried about you, Ana. You never answering your telephone.

ANA: I been in the Budapest.

JOVANKA: Would you like to have one coffee?

ANA: I very busy now. I got some important company.

JOVANKA: Maybe next week?

ANA: I vill again be in the Budapest. *Ciao.* As the Italiano say. *Ciao.*

> *She shuts the door, then turns to* CATHERINE.

You see. Coming. Spying to laugh on me. Same ting she done vhen my husband vas dying. She try to make she is the big nurse, helping Ana. Calling all the time to hear some bad news. Alvays standing over the bed of my dying husband. She tink because she vas the Serbian she got more right to him than Ana. I fix her.

CATHERINE: Do you think maybe she's just trying to be your friend, Ana?

ANA: You do not know the Serbian. And you do not know the Jovanka. She acting very nicely: 'Hello, Ana. Hello Ana.' But she is the snake. I have known many Jovanka. I like you. I like your nature. But I vorry that you must to be so stupid. Is hurting me, this stupidity. Is because you are so trusty you do not see Jovanka is the nasty.

CATHERINE: But, Ana, do you think that you're maybe seeing a nasty that isn't there?

ANA: Listen. Before the var, vhen I am young girl and my daddy is still in the life. My mummy call to me.

ANA'S MOTHER *walks in, calling to her.*

MOTHER: Ana, you must to go into the Budapest. And don't come back vithout the fabric. You know vhich fabric I talking.

ANA *is still* ANA, *but seems like a little girl.*

ANA: But, Mummy—is so hard to find von such fabric—

MOTHER: Do not come back vithout. [*She turns to leave, but then turns back.*] And don't talk to no von stranger in the Budapest. Look only after the fabric.

ANA'S MOTHER *leaves.* ANA *turns to* CATHERINE. *Like a young girl, she speaks to* CATHERINE.

ANA: Is most beautiful fabric anyvone can find—but is very hard to find—nearly impossible. Here I am, but I am the young girl. Long hair. Pretty. I vas like you. I did not know then I vas pretty. Valk vith me. I show you Budapest. Look, many people. You see, the street busy in the Budapest.

CATHERINE: Yes.

ANA: Nothing is blown in pieces yet. All is perfect still. Look, the people is happy. All except for little Ana, who can novhere find the fabric.

Something like time passes.

Very tired, the feet. Looking for hours and no fabric. Mummy never let me to come home, never anymore.

A man, ARTUR *is standing there.*

ARTUR: Hello, Ana.

ANA: Oh, is you! Artur. I did not recognise you. My mother's godson! I should to know you, straight avay!

ARTUR: I am looking different.

ANA *speaks to* CATHERINE.

ANA: Now for you, ve is speaking the English. So you can understand. But then it vas Hungarian ve vas speaking. He speak the English now even though he do not know it.

CATHERINE: That's nice of him.

ANA: But he do not see you.

CATHERINE: He doesn't?

ANA: No.

CATHERINE: Okay.

ARTUR: Vhat you doing in the Budapest, Ana?

ANA: Artur, I am in the bad. My mummy send me to find von fabric. Von very special fabric. I can no find. And you know Mummy.

ARTUR: Ja. I know your mummy. You is in the bad.

He winks at CATHERINE.

CATHERINE: Ana—you're wrong. He can see me.

ANA: Is no you he see. He tink you are me.

ARTUR *speaks to* CATHERINE *now, as though she is the young* ANA. *The real* ANA *steps slightly away.*

ARTUR: Ana, you vas in the bad, until you met Artur. I vill put you in the good.

CATHERINE *doesn't say anything.*

ANA: Ansver him.

CATHERINE: What do I say?

ANA: Use your brain. You vant to be the actress.

CATHERINE *speaks to* ARTUR.

CATHERINE: How can you help me?

ARTUR: I have this von. This fabric you vanting. I got.

CATHERINE: You have it?

ARTUR: Metre and metre. I got. Of the very special blue. Ink like midnight. But no star. Only butterfly. Vith the vings more big than your hand. Silver vings. On the butterfly.

CATHERINE: [*to* ANA] Is that what your mother wants?

ANA: Exactly! Exactly vhat vant my mummy!

ARTUR: Come. I take you. I sell to you for half price. Because your mummy is my godsmothers.

ANA *is speaking to* CATHERINE *as* ARTUR *leads her through Budapest.*

ANA: Go. Go. I go with him. Mummy vill be so happy on me. Ve go valking, valking. Through the Budapest. People everyvhere, but like shadows, because are strangers. You can no touch the stranger. Not anyvhere, my Kitty-kitty. Oh, Ana know this. You can no touch the shadow on the street no matter how is your lonely.

ARTUR *speaks only to* CATHERINE. *He no longer sees* ANA.

ARTUR: Is lucky for you I find you.
CATHERINE: Yes. Very lucky.
ANA: Here coming the tram.
ARTUR: Ve get on dis tram.

ANA *speaks to* CATHERINE.

ANA: You know tram. Like in the Melbourne. But open. No glass on vindow. Open, all of. And tram full of people.

CATHERINE *sits down.* ARTUR *sits next to her.*

ARTUR: And how is your father?
ANA: Good. At that time he vas.
CATHERINE: Good. He's good.
ARTUR: And your two sister?
CATHERINE: They're both good.
ANA: But von is little bit fatty.
ARTUR: And your von brother?
CATHERINE: Good too.
ANA: But he have the ugly girlfriend. Terrible ugly.
ARTUR: It's been too long since I vas in the town. Since I see your mummy.
ANA: Too long.
CATHERINE: Too long.
ANA: Ve miss him.
CATHERINE: We miss him—you.
ANA: Tram leaving city centre. And people get off.
CATHERINE: Do we get off here?
ARTUR: No, no, Ana. Soon.
ANA: Tram is now empty. How dat? Middle of the day and tram, empty, all of—and that vhen I hear it.
CATHERINE: Hear what?

ANA: You cannot hear? The voice?

CATHERINE: No. I don't hear any voice but yours.

ANA: That is very bad.

> *And suddenly, faster than* CATHERINE *can tell what is going on,* ANA *jumps off the tram. And she is gone.* CATHERINE *stands up, panicked, to look for her.*

ARTUR: No, Ana. Ve going further.

> *Not knowing what else to do,* CATHERINE *sits down next to* ARTUR *again.*

I miss the town, Ana. Sometimes is so lonely here in the Budapest. Many people, but vhen you can no touch them, talk them, they is only shadows on the street. I am glad I see you, Ana.

CATHERINE: You should come back home, to the town, Artur.

ARTUR: No. Is too late.

CATHERINE: Too late to come home?

ARTUR: For me. Vhat can a man like me do in the town? But here I is lost in the city. Vhere vill I go, Ana? Come. Here is our stop.

> *They get off the tram. They walk down a shadowy street.*

Is getting dark. Your mummy vill be vorry. I should to have told you to come back morning.

CATHERINE: Mummy will be happy. Because I will bring back the fabric.

ARTUR: Yes. Only a little further. Ve go to von factory. Only place is big enough to store such a lot of this fabric.

CATHERINE: These factories look very empty.

ARTUR: Many lose the business. Here ve are, Ana.

CATHERINE: But it's so dark in here.

ARTUR: Vhen ve are inside, the silver butterfly make the everyting light. Come.

> *They walk down the long, dark stairs.*

I remember you vhen you is even littler girl, Ana. You alvays playing vith the froggy. You alvays catch and your mummy scream on you.

CATHERINE: I've always loved the frog.

ARTUR: Ja. I don't love the frog.

CATHERINE: No?

ARTUR: I hate it. I hate the frog.

CATHERINE: Why?

ARTUR: Because is so noisy. And eat all of the butterfly. Sit down, Ana.

CATHERINE: Where is the butterfly fabric, Artur?

ARTUR: You didn't catch it? Frog ate. Frog ate all of. Ana's frog.

CATHERINE: I have to go.

ARTUR: No, Ana. You vill not be going.

CATHERINE: Mummy will worried.

ARTUR: Ja. She should to be. She vill not be seeing Ana never anymore. [*He has an axe.*] This is no because I don't like you, Ana. You vas alvays the good girl. I just don't have novhere else to go.

He begins to walk towards her, the axe raised.

CATHERINE: No—no! Help!

ANA*'s voice:*

ANA: You see now vhy you must not to be so trusty?

CATHERINE: Ana! Ana!

ARTUR: Yes, Ana.

ANA: You have learnt now the lesson?

CATHERINE: Yes! Yes!

ANA: Promise?

CATHERINE: I promise! I promise!

Just then ARTUR *lunges with the axe and* ANA *pulls* CATHERINE *away. They run, disappearing together.* ARTUR*'s voice calls desperately after them:*

ARTUR: Ana? Ana? Ana?!

CATHERINE *and* ANA *run down the street, holding hands.*

CATHERINE: Ana—you left me—

ANA: I teaching you the sixth sense, Kitty-kitty. I hear a voice vhen I still on the tram. [*Her voice booms out:*] 'Go back! You must to go back! Do not go vith the Artur. You vill die! Go back!' And Ana jump from the tram. But Kitty-kitty do not hear this voice because Kitty-kitty is too much the trusty. Trusting the Artur like she trusting the Jovanka. I teaching you.

CATHERINE: Artur was sick—

ANA: Ja. He vas the serial killer. He vas hang. In front of town. Mummy very sorry she vas his godsmothers.

CATHERINE: You left me with a serial killer?

ANA: Ja. Teaching. To save your life von day.

CATHERINE: But he wanted to kill me.

ANA: Many people vill vant to kill you. Better you is ready.

> CATHERINE *stops running. She looks around.* ANA *stops with her.*

CATHERINE: Ana—where are we?

ANA: Ve are on the Mary Street. In my lounges room. Vhere you tink?

CATHERINE: It's so different… It's so different to Hungary. Mary Street is so different to Budapest.

ANA: Ja. Too different.

CATHERINE: You were there. And now you're here. Ana.

ANA: Ja. Ana is here.

> *They are quiet for a moment.*

You vill stay here tonight. It is very late.

CATHERINE: Oh no, I better go home.

ANA: Dangerous. I don't vant the policeman come knocking on my door, say, 'Did you know dis girl?' I vill collapse.

CATHERINE: I won't get killed going across the street.

ANA: Don't be the trusty. Ja. I got the very good pyjama.

> ANA *takes out some satin pyjamas, hands them to* CATHERINE.

CATHERINE: Where will I sleep?

ANA: Vith the Bella, in dis room. You sleep vith the Bella. Very safety.

> ANA *puts* CATHERINE *to bed.*

END OF ACT ONE

ACT TWO

SCENE ONE

An infirmary, Hungary, just at the end of World War Two.

YOUNG ANA *is working in the infirmary. Tending to the injured soldiers. With a handkerchief tied over her face.*

A SOLDIER *is lying on the floor. It looks as though he is dead. He is lying on his back, on the floor. A blanket up to his chin.* YOUNG ANA *leans over him. She touches him lightly—thinking he is dead. She is about to pull the cover up over his face, when he grabs her arm, from the beneath the blanket where he lies.*

SOLDIER: Young girl. Young girl. Lift your handkerchief, young girl. Show me your face.

> YOUNG ANA *hesitates. And then lifts the handkerchief.*

You is the beautiful young lady. Vhy do you hide your face?

YOUNG ANA: Mummy say better the soldier do not see I is the young girl.

SOLDIER: Tell me… Var is finish?

YOUNG ANA: Yes.

SOLDIER: Young lady. Beautiful young lady. Please…

YOUNG ANA: Yes?

> *He is in terrible pain.*

SOLDIER: Please. Hold my legs. Hold my legs. Please. Hold my legs.

> *She lifts the blanket. But then stops.*

YOUNG ANA: I cannot. Your legs is gone.

SOLDIER: Gone… My legs is gone…

YOUNG ANA: Gone.

SOLDIER: But I feel them. Hurting. Show me.

YOUNG ANA: No. Don't look.

> *She touches his arm.*

Tell me. Vhat happen.

SOLDIER: I vas standing, at end of var. Standing vith von German soldier. In the snow. German soldier tell me to shoot into von town. I say, 'No. My mummy and daddy live in this town.' So German soldier turn and shoot me. All over the legs. And leave me to die in the snow. Coming von Russian soldier. He find me bleeding to death in the snow. And he carry me. On his back. I don't know how far. But vas for nothing.

YOUNG ANA: Not for nothing.

He grabs her hand.

SOLDIER: I feel it. My blood is gone.

A stern voice calls out.

VOICE: Girl. Girl. Come.

YOUNG ANA: I must to leave you. I am sorry.

VOICE: Girl!

SOLDIER: Please. I ask you. Go to my mummy and daddy. You must to travel far. Go to my mummy and daddy. And tell them I has died.

YOUNG ANA: You vill not dying.

SOLDIER: Young girl. Vhat is your name?

YOUNG ANA: Ana.

SOLDIER: Ana. You must to promise. To tell my mummy and daddy their son has died. Please.

VOICE: Girl! Ve going!

YOUNG ANA: Yes. I promise.

She has to leave.

Time and distance pass.

YOUNG ANA *arrives at a river. There is a* RUSSIAN SOLDIER *there with a gun and a raft. He holds the gun up to her. Right up to her head.*

Don't shoot. Don't shoot. Don't shoot.

RUSSIAN SOLDIER: Vhat you vant, Hungarian girl?

YOUNG ANA: This raft vill cross the river?

RUSSIAN SOLDIER: Da.

YOUNG ANA: Take me on your raft.

RUSSIAN SOLDIER: Is only to take Russian soldier across.

YOUNG ANA: You must to take me.

He still has the gun pointed at her.

RUSSIAN SOLDIER: I take you on raft, I don't need to shoot you. You vill drown.

YOUNG ANA: No. Not Ana.

RUSSIAN SOLDIER: You are swimmer?

YOUNG ANA: No. Never.

RUSSIAN SOLDIER: Then you are crazy.

YOUNG ANA: You vill take me?

RUSSIAN SOLDIER: Da. But if you falling, girl, you is lost.

> YOUNG ANA *holds onto the raft. They sail across the raging river.* YOUNG ANA *is nearly thrown from the raft, but her face has all the determination of* ANA *now, and she never lets go. They get to the other side.*

Vhere you going?

YOUNG ANA: To find the parents of von young man I know vonce.

RUSSIAN SOLDIER: He is dead? You cross this river for a dead man? You is brave Hungarian girl. Or maybe stupid. I see you when you come back this way.

> *She walks on. More time and distance pass.*

> YOUNG ANA *arrives at a door. She hesitates for a moment. And then knocks. A woman, the* SOLDIER'S MOTHER *answers.*

SOLDIER'S MOTHER: Hello?

YOUNG ANA: It has taken me too long to come. It took me too long to get the permission. You have waited too long to know. I have come to tell you, your son is died.

> *The* SOLDIER'S MOTHER *looks deeply into* YOUNG ANA.

SOLDIER'S MOTHER: Come inside.

> YOUNG ANA *enters their home. The* SOLDIER'S FATHER *is there.*

She know our son. She come to tell us he has died.

SOLDIER'S FATHER: Did you sit vith my son vhile he die?

YOUNG ANA: No. I vant to. But I am moved to different infirmary. I don't vant to go. But I must to. I vant to stay vith your son vhile he is dying.

SOLDIER'S FATHER: You is a good girl.

SOLDIER'S MOTHER: You vill stay for dinner.

YOUNG ANA: Tank you.

The table is already set with three places. The MOTHER *begins to set a fourth.*

You got three already.

SOLDIER'S MOTHER: Ja.

The MOTHER *sits. The* FATHER *sits.* YOUNG ANA *sits. And then a clomping sound on the floor. The Hungarian* SOLDIER *comes, walking very slowly on two heavy, iron legs. And he sits down with them, to dinner.*

YOUNG ANA *looks up at him. She loses her breath.*

YOUNG ANA: You're in the life…

He and YOUNG ANA *stare at each other. But then he looks down at his place and will no longer make eye contact.*

The evening has passed. And YOUNG ANA *and the* SOLDIER *are alone. He still won't look at her. She sits, looking right into him.*

I thought you vas died.

SOLDIER: Same Russian soldier that carry me on his back in the snow give me transfusion of his own blood. It keep me in the life. He should to have kept his blood.

YOUNG ANA: He save your life.

SOLDIER: Now he ferry the people across the river. He take me across vhen I come home.

YOUNG ANA: He ferry the people…

SOLDIER: He only meant to ferry the other Russian soldier. But he take many Hungarian too. He vill do this until he drown.

YOUNG ANA: He is the good man. Vhat he has done.

SOLDIER: His good blood is vaste on me. I am sorry you come here for nothing.

YOUNG ANA: No. Not for nothing. Before I coming for nothing. Now I got someting.

He won't look at her. She sits, looking into him. Finally he takes something from a pocket and hands it to her.

She takes it. It is a photograph.

SOLDIER: It is me. Before the var.

YOUNG ANA: Yes.

SOLDIER: You see. You see me vith the legs?

YOUNG ANA: Yes. I see you. [*She stands up. She walks over to him, holding the photograph.*] You are not so different now.

SOLDIER: Ha. My mummy and daddy is very happy. That I am in the life. But vhat for? Vhat for I lose my legs, and vhat for I am still in the life? I just vant to know. For who I lose my legs? For who?

> YOUNG ANA *looks at him. She reaches down, and touches his face.*

YOUNG ANA: Maybe for me. Maybe for me you lose your legs.

> *She kisses him. He sits there, and then pulls back.*

SOLDIER: Don't be sorry for me.

YOUNG ANA: I'm not. I have fallen in love on you.

SOLDIER: Vhy you say that?

YOUNG ANA: Von hundred percent. I fall in love on you.

> *She kisses him again.*

I never kiss the man before. You is the first. You vill be my first for everything.

SOLDIER: How can I…? Vithout the legs…

YOUNG ANA: You vill see. Ve learning together.

> *They kiss.*

> YOUNG ANA *is leaving. By the river. The* SOLDIER *is there with her. This time, instead of the* RUSSIAN SOLDIER *standing by the raft, it is* ANA *from now. She watches them.*

You vill come to see me?

SOLDIER: Yes.

YOUNG ANA: You promise?

SOLDIER: Yes.

> *They kiss.*

> YOUNG ANA, *now* CATHERINE *again, gets on the raft beside* ANA. *They sail away, both watching him on the shore. He whistles sweetly, the sound drifting out to them, as they float away.* CATHERINE *speaks to* ANA, *as they stand on the raft together.*

CATHERINE: Did he come to see you?

ANA: Oh yes, my sveetheart. He come. I am vorking at the church, vith many other young girl. Vhen I hear him, coming on his iron legs—I

am so, so happy—you believe me, my sveetheart—I am so happy—
my heart is jump!

They get off the raft. CATHERINE, *as* YOUNG ANA, *begins to work
at the church. And in the distance there is a whistling sound and
the sound of iron legs slowly clomping up, along the path. She
looks up—recognising the sound. It is the* SOLDIER. *They smile at
each other. He is coming, he looks so hopeful, towards* CATHERINE
on his iron legs, whistling. CATHERINE *whistles back at him. They
laugh.*

One of the other girls working at the church looks up and sees
CATHERINE *and the* SOLDIER *about to meet each other. She laughs
and says loudly:*

GIRL: Ana, how is it you cannot find von man vith the legs?

The SOLDIER *stops. He and* CATHERINE *look at each other. He
looks down. And then begins to hobble, slowly, away.*

CATHERINE *goes to run after him.*

ANA: No, my sveetheart.

CATHERINE: I'll follow him—

ANA: No, my sveetheart. He is too shame to speak.

CATHERINE: I'll go to his house—

ANA: No. I never see him. Never anymore in the life.

CATHERINE: How come you didn't tell him? You didn't tell him that girl
was an idiot—and that you loved him—

ANA: It don't matter vhat I tink. It matter vhat he tink of hisself. And of
hisself, he vas forever in the shame.

CATHERINE: You should have gone after him.

ANA: Ana know. Ana know the man.

CATHERINE: How do you know, Ana? How do you know when you
should run after a man? When he needs you?

They are back in Ana's lounge room.

ANA: You just know. I play to you von song. Is only song I keep in the
English. Very good. Very artistical, the Vynette.

ANA *puts on an old record. Tammy Wynette's, 'Stand By Your Man'
begins to play.*

A knocking on the door.

Vhite?

ANA *opens the door. And there is* KEN.

The de-a-bet-ic. Kitty-kitty, it is the sick boy you live vith.

KEN *comes inside.*

KEN: Hey, Kitty-kitty. So this is where you've been. Nice music.

CATHERINE: What are you doing here?

KEN: I thought you should know my diabetes has gotten a bit bad. I've been having some really full-on hypos.

CATHERINE: I didn't know that.

KEN: You haven't been home. Have you been staying here?

CATHERINE *looks sheepish.*

I had a really big hypo last night. The worst one yet. I wasn't in my head. I called my mother. And she called the police.

CATHERINE: She called the police?

KEN: Yeah. Because when I called her, I was driving.

CATHERINE: Oh, no.

KEN: She told them my number plate and the make of the car. When the police found me, I was parked, just sitting there, eating a muesli bar.

CATHERINE: You could have died.

KEN: Or I could have killed someone. Either way, we wouldn't have gotten to the end of the 'West Wing' together.

CATHERINE: That would be terrible. Are you okay now?

KEN: Yeah. I'm okay.

ANA *steps between them.*

ANA: Kitty-kitty, you no make the introduction?

CATHERINE: Ken, this is Ana. Ana, this is Ken.

ANA: Is my pleasure to meet you finally, Ken.

KEN: Likewise. It's great to finally meet Catherine's new best friend.

ANA: The Kitty-kitty talk about you all the time.

KEN: She does?

CATHERINE: I do?

ANA: All the time the Kitty say she love you. She love you. Ja. She tell me many time. I only vant to look after the poor, sick di-a-bet-ic.

CATHERINE: Ana—

ANA: She love you. She all the time love the de-a-bet-ic. Ja, she tell me many time. She. Love. You. I get the three coffee.

ANA *walks out of the room. It is just* KEN *and* CATHERINE *now.*

KEN: Hey, Catherine?

CATHERINE: Yeah?

KEN: Did you really tell Ana that you love me?

CATHERINE: Of course not.

KEN: I didn't think so.

CATHERINE: I don't know why she did that. Usually everything she says makes sense. But as if I'm in love with you.

She suddenly senses that he is hurt. She looks up.

I didn't mean it like that—

KEN: That's okay, I find you repulsive too.

CATHERINE: Really?

KEN: Yeah, you're pretty fat now that you eat. And you still have orange skin. As if I'd love you.

CATHERINE: As if!

KEN: Of course I love you.

CATHERINE: I can't.

KEN: Why?

CATHERINE: You're my friend. I need you to be my friend.

KEN: Right. Kind of like a butler.

CATHERINE: Like a butler?

KEN: Hanging around, waiting on you—organising your life—you don't even notice me. I'm the invisible hired help.

CATHERINE: Well, you're not hired. I don't pay you.

KEN: I'm not joking.

CATHERINE: I'm not laughing. Stop feeling sorry for yourself because you set up a situation where I would need you. Because you need to feel like you're running my life. And then feel sorry for yourself because I'm not in love with you. I never moved in here under the premise that I was in love with you.

CATHERINE *looks anxiously into her phone.*

KEN: Feel sorry for myself? You're one to talk.

CATHERINE: What?

KEN: Why are you staring into your phone, Catherine? Who do you hope is going to call you?

CATHERINE: I don't know.

KEN: You're waiting for him to call you, aren't you?

CATHERINE: No.

KEN: You are, Cathy—

CATHERINE: Don't.

KEN: You're not moving on with your life.

CATHERINE: I am.

KEN: You're not. Look—after all that's happened—and you're waiting for him to call you. It's not normal. I'm here, Catherine. I am right here.

CATHERINE: No you're not. You're in there. In the World of Warcraft or in the 'West Wing'—but you're not here. So you can't tell me to be here.

KEN: I would be if you were.

CATHERINE: Why does everyone want the one thing that's impossible?

KEN: You're waiting for Martin. And he's never coming.

CATHERINE: Why can't you just be my friend?

KEN: Is that really what you want?

CATHERINE: Yes.

KEN: Then I have to move out.

CATHERINE: What?

KEN: Well, I can't live with you like this.

CATHERINE: Oh, great—so I move in here with you—and you're meant to be my friend—and you make it okay to need you—and then the minute that you find out your fantasy isn't going to work, you give up on me.

KEN: I'm sorry you see it that way.

CATHERINE: I don't want you to move out.

KEN: You're never there anymore anyway, Catherine. You're always here. Hiding out with this old lady.

CATHERINE: I'm not hiding.

KEN: The thing is, it actually makes sense for me to go and stay at my mum's for a bit. She's really worried about my hypos. She keeps talking about me slipping into a coma.

CATHERINE: Are you going to slip into coma?

KEN: No. But I might lose a leg or two.

CATHERINE: I guess you can work on your film from there.

KEN: Yeah, sure.

CATHERINE: Or play World of Warcraft.

KEN: I've got a lot of people depending on me for a big raid coming up.

CATHERINE: You won't let them down.

> KEN *leaves.*

Ana!

> ANA *comes back in, with the tea trolley.*

ANA: [*very innocently*] Ja?

CATHERINE: Why did you tell the Ken I love him?

ANA: No!

CATHERINE: You told him I love him!

ANA: Ja. Like friend. Friend.

CATHERINE: You didn't say it like friend.

> ANA *almost looks sheepish for a moment, and then rallies.*

ANA: Is my broken English!

CATHERINE: Ana—

ANA: You should to run after him.

CATHERINE: You don't understand.

ANA: Ana understand. But perhaps Kitty-kitty no understand vhy Ana cannot follow this young soldier vithout the leg?

CATHERINE: Sometimes it's just impossible. Is that right?

ANA: Many time. But then you find the right. I find Vladir. Who you find? The homosexual? I joking! I joking. I like to ask you von very important favour. Because you are my friend. And I got no-von.

CATHERINE: Yes?

ANA: You is free tomorrow?

CATHERINE: Yes.

ANA: I like you coming vith me to the appointment with the Doctor Vhite. Very important. You vill come?

CATHERINE: Yes.

ANA: You promise you vill not be late?

CATHERINE: I promise.

ANA: I vill be in the shame if you cancelling.

CATHERINE: Ana, I won't cancel.

ANA: Should to be here tomorrow morning, no later than ten o'clock. Ve catching the bus.

SCENE TWO

CATHERINE *walks outside. There is* MARTIN, *with a suitcase.*

CATHERINE: Where are you going?

MARTIN: I'm catching the train to Brisbane.

CATHERINE: Why?

MARTIN: It's just for a little while.

CATHERINE: But why Brisbane?

MARTIN: It's more that I feel like going on a really long train ride.

CATHERINE: Don't do this.

MARTIN: Do what? You always get so dramatic. See the bigger picture. I'm just going to Brisbane.

CATHERINE: I can't stand it if you go again.

MARTIN: Before, you didn't even want to see me.

CATHERINE: I was wrong. Don't go.

MARTIN: I could use some help packing. Can you help me iron? I've got this idea, that I'd like to iron my suit. So that when I show up in Brisbane, it's like I'm a new man. Like anything's possible, you know? Would you iron my suit, Cathy?

> CATHERINE *doesn't answer him.*

Please, Cathy. I need your help.

> CATHERINE *doesn't answer.*

> *She begins to iron his suit.*

> *Meanwhile,* ANA *is by herself waiting on the street.* JOVANKA *walks down the street towards her.*

JOVANKA: Hello, Ana.

ANA: Jovanka.

JOVANKA: I hear the movie *Mamma Mia* very good. We go sometime together and have one coffee?

ANA: I don't like such silly tings.

JOVANKA: Where you going now?

ANA: To see Doctor Vhite. The Kitty-kitty take me there. She is the very good friend.

JOVANKA: Ja, good.

> JOVANKA *begins to head towards Katrina's house.*

ANA: And vhere you going?

JOVANKA: To the Katrina's.

ANA: You know the Katrina?

JOVANKA: Ja! I meet her on the street many time when I come to visit you, but you is busy. She invite me for the coffee.

ANA: She invite you for the coffee?

JOVANKA: Ja. Very nice voman. Many good recipe she lend me.

ANA: Go then to see her recipe.

JOVANKA: I call you later?

ANA: I vill not be home.

> JOVANKA *goes inside Katrina's house.* ANA *remains on the street.*
>
> KEN *begins to come out to his car, carrying boxes.*
>
> CATHERINE *is slowly ironing the suit.*

CATHERINE: Do you like creases in the pants?

MARTIN: Not really. But maybe it's better. Like more proper, you know?

CATHERINE: You don't have to be proper.

MARTIN: It's good sometimes. For a man to stand up.

CATHERINE: Help me iron.

MARTIN: How?

CATHERINE: Stand behind me.

> *He stands behind her.*

MARTIN: Like this?

CATHERINE: No. Like this.

> *She runs his hands over her. She guides him to stand close behind her, with his hands over hers on the iron. They iron slowly.*

You can be whatever kind of man you want. Just don't leave.

MARTIN: It's just Brisbane.

CATHERINE: What did I do? What did I do to make you go?

MARTIN: Nothing. You think too much, Cathy.

CATHERINE: I'm going to come with you this time.

MARTIN: What will you do there?

CATHERINE: I love Brisbane. We can go to Sea World. I don't need to pack. I'll just come. Now.

MARTIN: The train isn't until tonight. I'll meet you at the streetlamp just before the woods. You know, the flickering one.

CATHERINE: Yes. The flickering one. And we'll go from there?

MARTIN: Yeah.

She turns around and kisses him.

CATHERINE: Kiss me back.

MARTIN: I was.

CATHERINE: Kiss me like you're not somewhere else.

They kiss.

That's right—like you're here.

They kiss again.

It's not going to end this time.

They kiss, holding each other so tight. They continue to be wrapped up tightly in each other.

ANA *is standing on the street. Still waiting.* KEN *is packing his car. He drops his 'West Wing' DVDs.*

KEN: Shit!

He bends down and begins to pick them up, checking if they are scratched. He looks up and sees ANA, *waiting on the street.*

Hi, Ana.

ANA: Hello, Ken.

KEN: What are you doing? Do you need a lift somewhere?

ANA: The Kitty-kitty coming. Ve going very important appointment.

KEN: I can give you a ride.

ANA: No. Kitty coming.

KEN: Okay, see you later.

KEN *leaves.*

CATHERINE *and* MARTIN *make love.*

ANA *is still standing out on the street.* JOVANKA *and* KATRINA *bring their coffees out onto the street.*

ANA *hears them.* JOVANKA *sees* ANA *is still out there.*

JOVANKA: Ana! You is still waiting for the Kitty?

ANA: No. I is going.

ANA *walks off.*

SCENE THREE

ANA *sits across from* DOCTOR VHITE, *in her surgery.*

DOCTOR VHITE: And how is Bella, Ana?

ANA: The Bella very good, Doctor Vhite. And your three daughter?

DOCTOR VHITE: My daughters are fine, Ana.

ANA: The youngest? How is the youngest?

DOCTOR VHITE: She's very well.

ANA: She is the bastard.

DOCTOR VHITE: Pardon me?

ANA: No, not badly. Just the vay she is born. After you is already divorce. Ana remember. Hard life for the bastard.

DOCTOR VHITE: And how is your garden, Ana?

ANA: Too good.

DOCTOR VHITE: You must give me your gardener's number some time. I would love to have him look at my roses.

ANA: He is very expensive. Is hard for divorced lady like you to pay for someting so much. Better he is not looking after your roses.

DOCTOR VHITE: As you wish, Ana.

ANA: No, no, it is not me who vish it. I am looking after you. My husband—you remember the Vladir?

DOCTOR VHITE Yes. Of course. I was his doctor for fifteen years.

ANA: He tell me all the time, look after the people. He never know you are my doctor now.

DOCTOR VHITE: I'm sure he'd be very happy.

ANA: I don't tink so.

DOCTOR VHITE: I see.

ANA: He vas the private gentlyman. Very serious.

DOCTOR VHITE: Yes.

ANA: All the time he looked good bugger. Never show his age. Even vhen dying.

DOCTOR VHITE: It's easy for men.

ANA: Ja! Easier for the man. You are better for the divorce, Doctor Vhite. You are better now to be alone. You got the three daughter. They can help vith this, carry dat. You vill never be too lonely. Ana never had the childer.

DOCTOR VHITE: I know.

ANA: Ana only had Vladir. You know vhat he calling me—?

DOCTOR VHITE: His sweet Parishka.

ANA: He tell you dat?

DOCTOR VHITE: You did. After he died.

ANA: Don't keep the secret over me forever, Doctor Vhite.

DOCTOR VHITE: What do you mean?

ANA: You got the secret. Ana know this. Right now you are the secret vasp, because you got the secret sting for Ana.

DOCTOR VHITE: I don't understand.

ANA: Ja. You know. You is not the stupid, Doctor Vhite. My husband, he alvays say, vhat a pretty, intellygent voman is the Vhite. He all the time taking the showver before he come for the appointment. Vhy he take the showver before visiting the doctor? My husband never do that vhen the doctor is the man. Ja, Ana know. Don't keep anymore the secret over me.

DOCTOR VHITE: What do you want to know, Ana?

ANA: Don't vorry Doctor Vhite. Ana only vant to know the news. The news of vhat you got written on your papers. The news of vhat happen now vith Ana.

> DOCTOR VHITE *looks down at the medical papers. She looks back up and speaks to* ANA.

DOCTOR VHITE: The cancer has spread. It's in your stomach. It's in your liver. And it's in your lungs.

ANA: I vill dying?

DOCTOR VHITE: Yes, Ana. I'm afraid it doesn't look good. Why did it take you so long to come and see me?

ANA: I vas too busy in the life to be hearing your bad news.

> ANA *stops. She rights herself. She will not show emotion in front of* DOCTOR VHITE. *She begins to collect her bag, her coat.*

Tank you, Doctor Vhite. Tank you for your time.

DOCTOR VHITE: I'm sorry, Ana. I suggest we book you into a hospice as soon as possible.

ANA: That vill not be necessary.

DOCTOR VHITE: I won't be making any house calls, Ana. You'll need a hospice.

ANA: Vhat for? To be under the control? All her life Ana been the prisoner, and now Ana should to be the prisoner even in her death? No. Not

Ana. Ana stay vith the Bella. Good afternoon, Doctor Vhite. You should to be proud. You deliver first the news of my husband's death and now of Ana's. You kill us both, Vhite. Good. Better I go vith him.

SCENE FOUR

ANA *walks alone, back to Mary Street. She talks to her husband Vladir as she walks.*

ANA: You vas the lucky Vladir. You all the time had Ana. Vhen you is sick, vhen you is dying, you got Ana. Ana got no-von. Solo una Ana. Vhen you is dying and I is bathing your overhead, kissing your hands, carrying you on my shoulder, vashing your kaka, drying your pee-pee, you is very grateful. You is very grateful that I never say it. That I never say, 'Vhere are your other ladies now? Vhere is your doctor prostitute now?' No-von do that for you. No-von but Ana. Solo una Ana. You is very grateful, Vladir.

    She gets back home.

No matter. Ana vill fix. Keep going. Solo una Ana.

    CATHERINE *is just getting home too.*

Hello, Kitty-kitty.

CATHERINE: Hi, Ana.

ANA: You forget.

CATHERINE: What did I forget?

ANA: Oh, ho ho ho.

CATHERINE: The doctor's.

ANA: No matter.

CATHERINE: I'm sorry, Ana.

ANA: I am very sad.

CATHERINE: I really am sorry.

ANA: You come inside. Have von coffee.

CATHERINE: I can't right now. I have to get some stuff ready.

ANA: Oh, you is the busy?

CATHERINE: Yes.

ANA: Ah, good.

CATHERINE: Good what?

ANA: I catch someting.

CATHERINE: What?

ANA: Ja. You is getting fatty.

CATHERINE: Where?

ANA: The bum. Pulling you. Grown very much. And you has been vith the man. Vhen I vas needing you.

CATHERINE: I'm sorry, Ana. But it was very important.

ANA: Very important to be vith the dead boy.

CATHERINE: What?

ANA: You tink I don't see vith my ultrasound, Kitty love, the dead boy? Like idiot she vaiting for the ghost.

CATHERINE: Shut up.

ANA: Shut up… You tell Ana to shut up… You don't tell Ana to shut up. You shut up. Again, Ana can trust no-von. I should to know better. That you is the stupid young girl—making the sex vith the ghost. Vhy I tink you understand anyting? It is Ana who is stupid. But coming the change. Go, Kitty-kitty. Never come here. Never anymore.

CATHERINE: Ana—

ANA: Go! Go or I tell the Bella to killing you—go, Kitty-kitty!

> CATHERINE *runs from* ANA, *back into her own house, where there is no* KEN.
>
> *Meanwhile,* ANA *is speaking to herself. Speaking to Mary Street. Speaking to the world.*

Ana is all the time Ana. Solo una Ana! Solo una Ana. Solo una Ana. Solo una Ana. Solo una Ana. Solo una Ana. Solo una Ana. Solo una Ana. Solo una Ana. Solo una Ana. Solo una Ana. Solo una Ana.

SCENE FIVE

CATHERINE *stands under the flickering streetlamp.* MARTIN *is nowhere to be seen.*

She takes out her mobile phone. There is nothing on it—no message, no ringing. She looks around for him. She dials the number. It rings out. She dials again. She dials again and again. Finally she leaves a message in his voicemail.

CATHERINE: Martin? Martin! Martin! Where are you? You can't do this— you can't do this—

She hangs up. Dials again. Again. Message bank.
I hate you. I hate you.

SCENE SIX

The neighbourhood begins again.

ANA *stands out on the street. She is very feeble. Her illness has come upon her, quite suddenly. She looks in her wheelie bin.*

ANA: Again vith the nappy. Terrible cruelty.

KATRINA *is out on her porch.* ANA *waves eagerly.*

Hello, Katrina!
KATRINA: Hi, Ana.

KATRINA *goes back inside.*

The SAFEWAY DELIVERY BOY *shows up with bags.*

ANA: Safevay home delivery?
DELIVERY BOY: That's right, ma'am. You don't have as much as normal.
ANA: I lose the appetite.
DELIVERY BOY: No watermelon?
ANA: No. No vatersmelon.

He is gone. NANCY *comes along, handing out flyers.*

NANCY: Hi, Ana? Flyer for the next Neighbourhood Watch meeting?
ANA: No. I can no come.
NANCY: Really? I heard you were going to make Hungarian doughnuts.
ANA: Bastard baby horse.
NANCY: Pardon?
ANA: No. I vill not make it.

It is night. ANA *is at home, all alone. She is coughing. It is so obvious now, that she is very ill. A knock on her door. She stands, and moves slowly to go and answer it.*

Kitty?

But when she opens it, there is KATRINA.

KATRINA *doesn't look well. There is blood dripping down her face.*

Katrina.

KATRINA: I'm sorry. Sometimes I drop things. Sometimes I drop things and make a lot of noise.

ANA: You got the blood.

ANA *helps her inside.*

KATRINA: You see they took a hole—the size of a golf ball out of my head. And now sometimes I drop things and sometimes I forget people's names. Because of the cancer. It was in my brain. So sometimes I drop things… And sometimes I forget people's names…

KATRINA *doesn't notice the blood dripping into her eye.* ANA *reaches up, softly, and wipes it away with her sleeve.*

ANA: You felled down.

KATRINA: Sometimes I drop things. Sometimes I put things where they shouldn't go. Don't tell my daughter. Don't tell my son. I hope the cameras didn't catch it.

ANA: Now, Katrina, ve must to sit you down.

She goes into the bathroom, and takes out a small medical bag.

Ana can fix.

She gently tends to the wound on KATRINA*'s forehead.*

Both you and me, Katrina. Ve are in the trouble bastards. But you is the younger. I am sorry for you.

KATRINA: Ana? What happened?

ANA: You felled down, Katrina.

KATRINA: I better go home. To bed.

ANA: Ve must to be strong, Katrina. Never let the vorld see ve is crying. That ve is sorry for ourselves. To be dying. My husband's funeral—I stand over his coffins. Never to sit. Not for entire funeral. I must to stand guard over his coffins.

KATRINA: I really have to go to bed, Ana.

ANA *keeps talking.*

ANA: The priest is talking. He say many vise ting. And the people—many peoples—many of my husband's countrymen—the Serbians—who never like Ana—because I am the Hungarian—because I am never belong to no von—they looks—all of them vith their eyes strong to my back. Strong to see—does she cry? All of them, vonder—does she cry? And oh ho ho! How the people are surprise—how they admire me vhen no von tear come down.

KATRINA: Are you so sure they admired you?

ANA: I svallow the frog. Ja, like Ana, you vill svallow the frog. No-von see your pain.

> KATRINA *has stood up. Feebly. Both she and* ANA *look so feeble.*

KATRINA: But you're wrong, Ana. You just don't seem to understand. I'm not like you at all. I can't listen to you talk anymore. Thank you for helping me. But I have to go to bed.

> KATRINA *feebly leaves.* ANA *stands all alone.*

SCENE SEVEN

Some time has passed. CATHERINE *comes into the chemist, wheeling a small suitcase. She has a prescription. The* CHEMIST, *the same young man as before, comes out.*

CHEMIST: Hi, Kitty-kitty.

CATHERINE: Hi.

CHEMIST: You don't look so good.

CATHERINE: Thanks.

CHEMIST: No problem. It's my job.

CATHERINE: I thought that was a doctor's job.

CHEMIST: Details, details. What's wrong with you?

CATHERINE: I've been staying at my parents' house.

CHEMIST: What have they been doing? Poisoning you?

CATHERINE: No. I got sick. And they were taking care of me. How come you're sunburnt?

CHEMIST: I went to Sea World.

CATHERINE: No way? I love Sea World!

CHEMIST: You do?

CATHERINE: Who doesn't? Did you swim with the dolphins?

CHEMIST: No. They were getting their vaccinations when I was there. I had to swim with the sharks.

CATHERINE: Really?

CHEMIST: Only the small ones.

CATHERINE: What a shame! I loved swimming with the dolphins there.

CHEMIST: You swam with them?

CATHERINE: Yeah. It was amazing.

CHEMIST: Can I show you something?

CATHERINE: Sure.

> *He takes out a photo from behind the counter. It is a picture of him superimposed on a dolphin, as though he is riding it.*

Oh, my God, you rode the dolphin!

CHEMIST: No, no, it's fake.

CATHERINE: Oh—so it is! What a great idea, though. If you can't swim with 'em, ride 'em.

> *They smile at each other.*

CHEMIST: How's your neighbour?

CATHERINE: Ana?

CHEMIST: Who else?

CATHERINE: She's good…

CHEMIST: Yeah. She's pretty cool. She gets around pretty well for such a sick old lady.

CATHERINE: Sick? Ana's sick…

> *The* CHEMIST *realises he's overstepped a bit.*

CHEMIST: You didn't know?

CATHERINE: How long has she been sick for?

CHEMIST: I shouldn't have said anything.

> CATHERINE *looks at his face.*

CATHERINE: Is she going to be okay?

> *The* CHEMIST *doesn't say anything.*

She's dying. Isn't she? Oh, shit.

CHEMIST: Well, the good news about Mrs Brajavik is, she only lives just down the road.

SCENE EIGHT

ANA *and* CATHERINE *arrive at the mall. This is the first time we've seen them together since the fight.* ANA *inspects* CATHERINE.

ANA: You looks good bugger. They vill be raping you.

CATHERINE: Thank you, Ana. You look good too.

ANA: I vear this red coats. Is only for special occasion. My husband's funeral and now the *Mamma Mia*.

> ANA *reaches into her handbag and pulls out two fifty-dollar bills, and holds them out to* CATHERINE.

CATHERINE: Ana! No!

ANA: I don't give to you. I vant you to handly my money. Today, I pay for everyting, but I never should to reach into my handsbag to handly the money in front of the Jovanka. Jovanka tell me she meet us in front of the Baker Delight downstair.

CATHERINE: Is this it?

ANA: Is it the Baker Delight?

CATHERINE: Yes.

ANA: Then she should to be here.

> *Just then,* JOVANKA *comes creeping along.*

There! There is the Jovanka! Ve catch her!

> CATHERINE *calls out.*

CATHERINE: Jovanka!

ANA: Shhh. Don't jump/

CATHERINE: /Jump. Yeah, yeah, I know.

ANA: She should to see us and come. Don't be the baby horse.

> JOVANKA *sees them and walks over.*

JOVANKA: Hello, Ana. Hello, Kitty-kitty. I walk all the vay from my house.

> *She is quite out of breath.*

CATHERINE: Oh, you must be exhausted.

ANA: She only live in the Bondi.

JOVANKA: I go fast. I did not want to be late.

CATHERINE: Don't worry, we've got forty minutes until it's on.

ANA: Kitty-kitty—you go to get the tickets [*whispering out the side of her mouth*] vith money I give you. Do not be taking no money from the Jovanka—and ve be sitting here.

> ANA *sits with her lips pursed, on one of those park benches that are kept inside shopping malls.* JOVANKA *sits down heavily next to her.*

CATHERINE: Okay. Back soon, ladies.

She arrives at the movie ticket booth. She speaks to the WOMAN *working there.*

Hello, I'd like three tickets to *Mamma Mia* for the one p.m. session please.

WOMAN: I'm sorry, there is no one p.m. session.

CATHERINE: What? What time is it on?

WOMAN: The only session today is at seven p.m.

CATHERINE: Seven p.m.! Listen, this is actually a very big problem. I have two old ladies with me—one of them is Hungarian, and the other is Serbian—she walked here—and they've come to see the one p.m. session.

WOMAN: Well, that is a problem because there isn't a one p.m. session.

CATHERINE: I need to speak to your manager. Because, I'm sorry, but that just isn't acceptable. I called just the other day and the message said *Mamma Mia* is on at one p.m. So something is going to have to be done about this.

WOMAN: First of all, I am the manager. Second, did you happen to listen to the part of the message that says the recording with the session times changes each Thursday?

CATHERINE: Um…

WOMAN: Well, today's Thursday.

CATHERINE: I see.

WOMAN: Yes.

CATHERINE: I'm very sorry about that.

WOMAN: Okay.

CATHERINE: What should I say to the old ladies?

WOMAN: Ask them if they want to see the seven o'clock session.

> CATHERINE *returns to* ANA *and* JOVANKA. *Neither of them have moved. They sit side by side, but with a big space between them on the indoor park bench.* JOVANKA *is still mildly out of breath and* ANA *is staring ahead, looking stoic.*

> ANA *sees* CATHERINE *coming.*

ANA: Ah. Here is my girl.

CATHERINE: Uh, Ana, could I have a word with you?

ANA: Vhat? Sit down.

> CATHERINE *sits between the two ladies on the bench.* JOVANKA *is listening too.* CATHERINE *looks extremely nervous.*

CATHERINE: Um, there's been a bit of a problem. With the tickets.

ANA: Problem. Vhat problem?

CATHERINE: There was a mix-up. The movie isn't until seven p.m…

> ANA *pauses for a moment. Considers this. And then says:*

ANA: Then ve vill come back seven p.m. [*She looks challenging at* JOVANKA.] Vill you be coming back for the *Mamma Mia* seven o'clock, Jovanka?

JOVANKA: Ja. I come back.

> ANA *speaks only to* CATHERINE, *who is in the middle of* ANA *and* JOVANKA.

ANA: I got a surprise. Vhen she say she be coming back seven o'clock. I got a surprise! I never tink she be coming back, no, no, no. But now carefully, she vill be inviting us to her home for von coffee. But ve vill not be going.

> ANA *has been speaking quite loudly. Loud enough so that* JOVANKA *could easily hear.* CATHERINE *looks at* JOVANKA *nervously, but she appears to have heard nothing.*

CATHERINE: We won't?

ANA: No! Vhy? Vhy should I to sit vhile she make herself very important, never offer no von biscuit, give the cold coffee, her husband laughing on me. No. Ve vill not be going to her house for von coffee.

JOVANKA: You come to my house for one coffee?

CATHERINE: Uh…

JOVANKA: Come for one coffee?

CATHERINE: Uh, Ana… Jovanka wants to know if we'd like to go to her house for one coffee.

ANA: No. No. Ve vill not be going.

> ANA *stares proudly, straight ahead.* CATHERINE *turns back to* JOVANKA.

CATHERINE: Uh, Jovanka, Ana says we're busy and can't come for the coffee.

JOVANKA: You come for one coffee?

CATHERINE: Um, Ana…

ANA: No.

CATHERINE: Uh, we can't make it for the coffee, Jovanka, but we'll meet you here later for the *Mamma Mia*.

ANA *and* CATHERINE *walk together along the street.*

Ana, I'm really sorry that you're dying.

ANA: Who tell you dat?

CATHERINE: I'm not telling you.

ANA: Good. You is learning.

CATHERINE: Let me teach you something too. Sometimes, Ana, if you look for the good it's there too. Your sixth sense saved you from the serial killer. It's saved your life many times. I know that. But sometimes, it would be better not to listen to it so much.

ANA: You mean I should to shut up sometimes.

CATHERINE: You know you should to.

ANA: I have had the very hard life.

CATHERINE: I know you have, Ana. You're still at war. In your mind, you're still at war.

ANA: Yes. I am still in the war.

CATHERINE: Your next-door neighbours who put dirty nappies in your bin aren't trying to kill you. Jovanka's not the Gestapo.

ANA: She is more vorse—

CATHERINE: You're a good person, Ana. A kind person.

ANA: Ja, ja.

CATHERINE: But your sixth sense sees the bad in people and you can't leave it alone.

ANA: I am the foxy!

CATHERINE: Too much you are the foxy. You would be happier if you were a little stupider.

ANA: Ja. Vould to be.

CATHERINE: You're my best friend, Ana, but you need more friends. You need some old bastards.

ANA: Ja. I need the old bastard.

CATHERINE: Give Jovanka a chance.

ANA: Even now I dying?

CATHERINE: Especially now that you're dying.

ANA: I like to tell you something, my sveetheart.

CATHERINE: Yes?

ANA: You ask von time. And now I like to tell you vhy I never had the childer. You vant to know?

CATHERINE: Yes.

ANA: Vhat you got to understand, my sveetheart, is that in life I got the two husband. Vladir and the first von. I marry first time very young.

CATHERINE: Did you love him?

ANA: No. But tings are different. Var just finish. Ve got nothing. I hardly know him. But ve marry.

> *Hungary begins to form around* ANA.

You see, Kitty-kitty. Ve live together this small house. More like hut. Is cold alvays. You feel dat?

CATHERINE: Yes. It's so cold.

ANA: And you see, he is not home.

CATHERINE: Where is he?

ANA: This man I marry, he is gone from home, very much.

CATHERINE: Do you miss him?

ANA: It hurt me. It hurting me that he gone for so much. And you know Ana. You know the sixth sense that Ana got. Pulling me. That something is not in the right.

CATHERINE: What is it?

ANA: Look in his coats pocket. Here.

> *She hands* CATHERINE *a man's coat.* CATHERINE *puts her hand in the pocket and takes out a piece of paper. She hands the piece of paper to* ANA.

Von address. I vill find. Must to travel to the next town.

> *She begins to travel.*

I am five month pregnant, at this time. But I don't have the money for the train. Ve got nothing. So I follow the train track ten kilometre to next town.

> ANA *walks, pregnant, along the train tracks.* CATHERINE *follows her.*

> *Finally they get there.* ANA *approaches a house. She leans against the rail, then straightens herself. She knocks on the door.*

> *A young man answers. A* POLICEMAN.

POLICEMAN: How may I help you?

ANA: I am looking for Moric Csazar.

POLICEMAN: He is not here.

ANA: You know vhere I find him?

POLICEMAN: He is vith my sister. On the holiday.

ANA: Vith your sister? Together?

POLICEMAN: Ja. He is her boyfriend.

> ANA *looks ill. He looks at her.*

ANA: That boyfriend of your sister, is my husband. [*She begins to walk back.*] You see? That police gentlyman? He is sorry for me?

> CATHERINE *looks back at him, then nods that yes, he is.*

I valk back. Ten kilometre on the train track. I have no money for the train.

> CATHERINE *follows her along the train tracks, but there is some distance between them.* ANA *is the* ANA *she was then. As she walks along the train tracks, she speaks.*

I tell to my mummy everyting. She take me to von man. Ve don't tell him that pregnancy is five month. Say two month. Or he never do. It cost von hundred egg.

He got no anaesthetic. He tie my arm up and my leg apart and vith his tools he do the abortion. I am bleeding to death. My mummy and sister take me out and lay me in the sun. They tink I vill be dying. But not Ana. Ana don't die. Keep going. My mummy say, better now, to leave the Hungary.

I leave. And they catch me on the border of Yugoslavia. And so I am the prisoner in the camp. And five year later, vhen I escape there, I am the prisoner in the Italiano camp. They keep me in the camp six-year there, because of my divorce, and they are the Catholic bugger. I escape again, to France. And two year later, they send me to the Austral. And then again the camp. Fourteen year, the camps for Ana.

CATHERINE: That's why you never had children.

ANA: I could not. My vomb, it vas finish in the abortion.

> ANA *and* CATHERINE *walk along the train tracks.* ANA *sings.*

> [*Sung*] All it cost von hundred egg, to cut you free from me,
> All it cost von hundred egg and, sveetheart, you are free.

> Five month from my heart, to delivery,
> Five month from my heart, to delivery.

> All it cost von hundred egg and, my sveetheart, you are free,
> All it cost von hundred egg, to cut you free from me.

All it cost von hundred egg, and sveetie, you are free.

Five month from my heart,
To delivery.

All it cost von hundred egg and, sveetie,
You are free.

> ANA *stops. She looks at* CATHERINE.

Kitty-kitty, this dead boy you love, he is no yours anymore. He is everybody's boy now. You must let him go free final and live your life. You understand?

CATHERINE: Yes, Ana. I understand.

ANA: Here ve are. Back for the *Mamma Mia*.

> *They look up at* JOVANKA *who is sitting all by herself. She sees them, her face lights up.*

JOVANKA: I tink you were not coming.

> ANA *speaks to* CATHERINE.

ANA: Quickly. Vith my money, you go to make the purchase. Three ticket. Von for you. Von for me. And von for Jovanka—bastard. Shh-shh-shhh.

> *They all sit watching the film.* ANA *talks all the way through it.*

Oh! Very artisical! She—the Streep—she is the very artistical! Oh, you hear vhat the boy say? Ho, ho, ho! You should to find von such a husband, Kitty-kitty. Very artistical, the *Mamma Mia*.

> *After the movie, as they come out of the cinema, holding their ice-creams,* JOVANKA *speaks to* ANA.

JOVANKA: You come for one coffee?

> ANA *pauses for a while. She looks at* CATHERINE. *Then she looks back at* JOVANKA.

ANA: Ja. I come for von coffee.

> ANA *and* JOVANKA *sip their coffees.* CATHERINE *sits with them.* ANA *finishes her coffee. She smiles at* JOVANKA. *Smiles at* CATHERINE. *She collapses.* CATHERINE *jumps up.*

CATHERINE: Ana.

> JOVANKA *rushes to* ANA's *side.*

JOVANKA: Ana! Ana!

> CATHERINE *kneels down beside her. Holding her.* JOVANKA *is still calling out to her:*

Ana! Ana!

> *The ambulance arrives. Two* AMBULANCE OFFICERS—*man and a woman.* CATHERINE *is still sitting, cradling* ANA. JOVANKA *is kneeling over her, crying.*

> *The* AMBULANCE OFFICERS *bend down, check* ANA*'s breathing, her pulse. They lift her up onto the stretcher.* CATHERINE *sees that one of the ambulance officers is* MARTIN.

CATHERINE: Hi.

MARTIN: Hi. I'm so sorry about your friend.

CATHERINE: Martin. Why did you kill yourself?

MARTIN: It was years ago now, Cathy.

CATHERINE: But why? Why did you do it?

MARTIN: I was so unhappy.

CATHERINE: What should I have done to make you happy?

MARTIN: You did everything you could do. You were a real friend.

CATHERINE: You and I, we'll never see each other again.

MARTIN: No.

> CATHERINE *kisses him on the cheek.*

CATHERINE: Look after her. Look after Ana.

MARTIN: I promise.

> MARTIN *and the other* AMBULANCE OFFICER *begin to carry* ANA *away.*

CATHERINE: Ana. Ana. Parishka. Don't worry. He'll look after you.

> *And they are gone.*

SCENE NINE

Some time has passed. CATHERINE *sits on the letterbox. She stares out into the street.*

KEN *comes and stands next to her.*

KEN: I'm back.

CATHERINE: Thank God.

KEN: They cured my diabetes.

CATHERINE: Really?

KEN: No, you idiot. But my blood sugar level is way better.

CATHERINE: That's so great. I deleted Martin's number from my phone. Any news on your film?

KEN: Roadshow have come on board and we start filming early next year.

CATHERINE: No way! You're lying.

KEN: It's true.

CATHERINE: How are you going to fit that in with World of Warcraft?

KEN: I had to delete it from my computer. It hurt. But in a good way.

CATHERINE: That's so great.

KEN: My aunt still wants to interview you. And I still want to be your friend. And possibly give you a screen test for my film.

CATHERINE: Really?

KEN: Yeah, of course. No promises.

> CATHERINE *is quiet. Then she smiles at* KEN.

CATHERINE: We're in the life, Ken.

KEN: In the life?

CATHERINE: Yeah.

> *A barking sound comes from their house.*

KEN: We even have a dog now. That's really being part of life.

CATHERINE: Do you mind?

KEN: No. At least with Bella I'll know my collector's edition of the entire 'West Wing' series will be safe. Speaking of which, I've got some spare time. In fact, I've got exactly forty-two minutes spare.

CATHERINE: Hey, isn't that the length of a 'West Wing' episode?

KEN: You have been paying attention.

> *They go to walk inside.*

Hey, happy Obama, my friend.

CATHERINE: Yeah. Happy Obama.

THE END

ALSO AVAILABLE FROM CURRENCY PRESS

Goodbye Vaudeville Charlie Mudd and Return to Earth
by Lally Katz

Set in Edwardian Melbourne, *Goodbye Vaudeville Charlie Mudd* is an evocation of a forgotten past—a play about pain and cruel desire; about the need for laughter, the palaces we build for it, and its human cost.

'A deeply accomplished work: darkly beautiful theatre that resonates in the intimate chambers of the mind.' *The Australian*

Return to Earth edges on the whimsical but is ultimately lyrical and profound. It is a poignant play that tenderly captures the moment, often littered with casualties, when a young person moves from transparency to opacity, from childhood to adulthood—a period of intense loss and confusion.

'The parallel universe of Lally Katz's imagination is an estranging, breathlessly anxious, uneasily hilarious place.' *The Australian*

ISBN 978 0 86819 938 2

Gwen in Purgatory
Tommy Murphy

Gwen is 90. She woke up this morning to discover that purgatory is sitting alone in a new house in a new subdivision on the edge of town, trying to work out if the remote in her hand operates the air-con or the fan-forced oven. But then her grandson turns up, and Father Ezekiel, a priest from Nigeria, arrives to bless the house, and the beginning of the end starts to look up. When more of Gwen's kids arrive, each with their own motives and demons, this family of ordinary souls must battle to keep faith, both with Gwen and each other.

'Tommy Murphy's new play is as deft and pungent a comedy as your are likely to see this year or any other … it already feels like a classic.' *Sydney Morning Herald*

ISBN 978 0 86819 894 1

.

www.ingramcontent.com/pod-product-compliance
Lightning Source LLC
Chambersburg PA
CBHW050019090426
42734CB00021B/3332